SEXUAL DISORDERS

PUBLISHING FOR THE WORLD
125 Years
THE JOHNS HOPKINS UNIVERSITY PRESS

SEXUAL DISORDERS

■ PERSPECTIVES ON

DIAGNOSIS AND

TREATMENT

Peter J. Fagan, Ph.D.

With a Foreword by Paul R. McHugh, M.D.

THE JOHNS HOPKINS UNIVERSITY PRESS
Baltimore and London

© 2004 The Johns Hopkins University Press
All rights reserved. Published 2004
Printed in the United States of America on acid-free paper
9 8 7 6 5 4 3 2 1

The Johns Hopkins University Press
2715 North Charles Street
Baltimore, Maryland 21218-4363
www.press.jhu.edu

All figures by Jacqueline Schaffer
Book design by Teresa Bonner

Library of Congress Cataloging-in-Publication Data

Fagan, Peter Jerome.
    Sexual disorders : perspectives on diagnosis and treatment /
Peter J. Fagan ; with a foreword by Paul R. McHugh.
        p. ; cm.
Includes bibliographical references and index.
    ISBN 0-8018-7526-9 (alk. paper) — ISBN 0-8018-7527-7 (pbk. :
alk. paper)
    1. Psychosexual disorders—Diagnosis.   2. Psychosexual disorders—
Treatment.   3. Sex therapy.
    [DNLM: 1. Sexual Dysfunctions, Psychological—diagnosis.
2. Sexual Dysfunctions, Psychological—therapy. WM 611 F151s 2003]
I. Title.
    RC556.F345 2003
    616.85'83—dc21

                                                        2003007657

A catalog record for this book is available from the British Library.

To my wife, Gail Lambers

CONTENTS

FOREWORD

Books on sexual pathology by psychologists and psychiatrists line library shelves. But I am repeatedly struck by how little most of these books teach about the specific character of the sexual difficulties patients bring to doctors. Many preach the same sermon: "You think you have a sexual problem but actually some deeper psychic conflict of yours has expressed itself as a sexual symptom." This "root cause" explanation draws attention away from the particular maladaptive conditions — holding out the promise that they are phenomena more like fever or cough that fade away as the more fundamental matters (i.e., the "root causes") are addressed.

This logical but in practice ineffective approach to maladaptions, including sexual ones, was challenged and eventually refuted as a therapeutic procedure by Alcoholics Anonymous (AA) in the 1930s. Then psychiatrists regularly sought some provocation or "root cause" for excessive drinking but often failed to help their alcoholic patients. AA proclaimed that alcoholism and its explanation were actually one and the same. Alcoholic persons will seldom recover by searching for some hidden provocative cause but will mend if they identify themselves as "alcoholics" vulnerable to losing control when drinking and therefore exert all their powers (and seek help from others) to stop drinking — "just for a day."

Actually there is no mystery behind the success of AA's approach. Alcoholism does have provocations or "roots," but drinking can quickly become a habit sustained by its rewarding consequences. By then, the provocations have faded in significance. Only a direct and systematic attack on alcohol consumption itself will help the alcoholic person recover.

Learning from this example, therapists should look at every other maladaptive activity directly, see it often as its own explanation, note especially how it has become a way of life for the patient, and then work diligently to discern what can be done to stop it. This idea certainly applies to sexual disorders. A sexual problem is first and foremost a sexual problem, not another problem in disguise. It follows, therefore, that those who would help a patient with a sexual problem must learn about the sexual problem "in itself," not as a symptom of something else.

Sexual Disorders teaches this message. In writing this book, Dr. Fagan has drawn on his experience directing the Sexual Behaviors Consultation Unit at Johns Hopkins, where patients suffering serious maladaptive sexual difficulties are investigated and treated. There Dr. Fagan came to see different classes of sexual problems whose different natures entailed different prognoses and treatments. This book distills his observations on this subject.

Dr. Fagan generously suggests that our book, *The Perspectives of Psychiatry* (Johns Hopkins University Press, 1998), helped him find a coherent structure from which to speak about the different kinds of sexual disorders. For this, I have a colleague's gratitude. But more to the point, I have learned much from Dr. Fagan. For example, with his help I can see how a sexual problem that emerges in the midst of a psychiatric disease such as bipolar disorder—manic type differs in treatment and prognosis from a paraphilic disorder emerging in an individual with an excitement-seeking, extraverted temperament. Thus, explanation and example emerge from his varied experiences in the clinic.

Perhaps existing treatises on sexual maladaptions promote the "root cause" approach because they believe it encourages nonjudgmental practices with patients, given its assumption of common human vulnerabilities and fellow feelings. This kindly intended idea expresses itself in the motto: "There but for the grace of God go I." But differentiating the sexual disorders according to their natures as Dr. Fagan does here protects equally well against the judgmental condemnation that is so adverse to a treatment alliance. It empathetically acknowledges the distressing diminution of choice provoked by the hungers that drive these tendencies. But it does more than identify and commiserate with the character of the lost freedom. It differentiates the fundamental natures of the different sexual maladaptions even as it describes the therapeutic approaches suitable to correct them. This stance of description, differentiation, and therapeutics also suggests appropriate paths for research into these disorders.

A crucial moral prevails here: we should scrutinize sexual disorders for themselves just as we scrutinize addictive disorders, eating disorders, and sleep disorders for themselves. As a result, our powers of understanding and treatment will increase. We need not fear that we will drift either toward reflexive condemnation that disrupts any therapeutic opportunity or into callous license that ignores the patient's need to regain the freedom lost to intemperate habit and dominating preoccupations.

I expect this book to become a model of its kind and ultimately bring clarity to an arena of psychiatry where, despite past interest and effort, little fundamental service to patients has emerged.

PAUL R. McHUGH, M.D.

ACKNOWLEDGMENTS

This book is the product of nearly two decades of collaboration with friends and colleagues at the Johns Hopkins University School of Medicine. I am grateful primarily to the persons with whom I have been privileged to work in the Sexual Behaviors Consultation Unit (SBCU) for twenty years. Chester Schmidt has given steady leadership to the SBCU since the early 1970s; he is always ready to identify questions raised by the clinical cases and to pose challenges for further research. It is impossible for anyone to be around Tom Wise, with his intellect and enthusiasm, and not be curious about the phenomenology of human sexuality and to pursue that curiosity in a rationally cohesive fashion. Julia Strand, when with us in the SBCU, was a partner in wondering about the complexities of the human psyche and the remarkable manner in which sexual behavior expresses this complexity. These three colleagues have been central to the development of my thought as reflected in this book.

In addition to the central roles played by Chet, Tom, and Julia, the SBCU has benefited from the presence of two leaders in the field of psychological measurement. Paul Costa is not only an international expert in personality but also, more importantly, a friend and colleague who generously collaborates with and teaches us. For more than thirty years, Len Derogatis has been the preeminent psychometrician in human sexuality. He was a mentor in my clinical psychology internship in the early 1980s and has been a professional colleague since then.

Others in the SBCU fostered the work of the unit and my ability to grow in an understanding of the various perspectives on human sexuality. They are Emile Bendit, Lois Blum, David Cowie, Ellen Halle, Linda Hellman, Van King, Chris Kraft, Dinah Miller, Yula Ponticas, Mark Reader, Linda Rogers, Lex Smith, Bob Ward, and Debbie Weaver. A special thanks to Cindy Osborne and Steve Johnson, who, as associate directors of my two "day jobs," provided the coverage necessary to give me the time to write the book.

For the past ten years I have organized the human sexuality curriculum for the first- and second-year medical students at Johns Hopkins—an eighteen-hour curriculum, generous by current medical school standards. This task has permitted me to be updated annually in the genetic and biological, medical, and psychosocial aspects of human sexuality by a wonderful interdepartmental faculty. Among the Hopkins faculty, I am grateful to Greg Ball, Lisa Beasley, Fred Berlin, Bud Burnett, Adrian Dobs, Leslie Heinberg, Alain Joffe, Jeremy Nathans, Bill Reiner, Courtland Robinson, Leon Rosenberg, and Julie Van Rooyen. In addition, Mike Plaut, of the University of Maryland School of Medicine, Sandy Lee, of Northern Virginia Family Services, and David Rowland, of Valparaiso University, generously traveled to Hopkins to teach us. Annually, the medical student lecturers taught the medical students well, and, in doing so, they taught this faculty member.

Over the past two decades, many persons have helped me think about what has emerged as the contents of this book, sometimes with a carefully designed research presentation at meetings of the Society for Sex Therapy and Research or the International Academy of Sex Research, at other times with a very brief comment made in passing. For their help in thinking about human sexuality and, in many cases, their enlightening presentations and publications, I especially thank Richard Friedman, Julia Heiman, Sandra Leiblum, Derek Polonsky, Ray Rosen, David Scharff, Raul Schiavi, Pat Schreiner-Engel, Taylor Segraves, Leonore Teifer, Ken Zucker, and the trio from Cleveland: Stan Althof, Steve Levine, and Candace Risen.

Others, professionally outside the field of human sexuality, were helpful at various stages in the writing of this book. For their comments and, most often, answers to my questions I am very grateful. I thank Andy Cherlin, Charles Curran, Hank Giedzinski, and Jennifer Haythornthwaite.

I am especially grateful to those who made helpful comments on preliminary drafts of the book: Tom Wise, Chet Schmidt, Melinda Fitting, and Julia Strand. Matt McDonald's encouragement was priceless.

I am grateful to the patients who entrusted to me and to all of us in the Sexual Behaviors Consultation Unit their sexual problems and concerns. Health, mental health, and sexual health are collaborative works of those who seek assistance and those who attempt to help. But the direction of the beneficence is not one way. I have been helped and taught by my patients, and I am grateful for the life wisdom they have provided. The cases described in this book are composites of those who have shared their life story as partners in achieving mental and sexual health. No one should be recognizable, even to himself or herself. The human condition is universal.

The graphic art of Jackie Schaffer has contributed to the understanding of the perspectives and how they might be integrated. I thank my editor at the Johns Hopkins University Press, Wendy Harris, whose quiet and consistent nudges were just what was needed.

I am, of course, very indebted to the work of Paul McHugh and Phillip Slavney in their *Perspectives in Psychiatry*. Without *Perspectives* and Paul's personal support, this book would not have been written.

While I am grateful to all the above and many others for their contributions to my thinking and to this book, all limitations and any errors contained herein are my responsibility.

Last, and most important, I thank my wife, Gail Lambers, for her protection of the time and space I needed to write this book and for the loving support that makes such work possible.

SEXUAL DISORDERS

■ 1

INTRODUCTION
TO THE PERSPECTIVES
ON SEXUAL DISORDERS

There is no lack of information about sex today. The media, the Internet, daily conversations are filled with sexual information and misinformation. When sexual behaviors become so problematic that an individual seeks or society demands professional treatment for the behavior, it is imperative that the clinician organize the mass of information available into a systematic way of thinking about sex. The four *perspectives* — disease, dimension, behavior, and life story — offer an epistemology, a way of thinking, about sexual disorders and disordered behaviors so that treatment can be rationally applied to the particular situation.

THE PERSPECTIVES

What are the perspectives? To answer this simply, the perspectives are four different ways of viewing a clinical case. The image of windows in a house, each of which looks out in a different direction, comes to mind. Perhaps even more apt is the story of the four blind men who touch the trunk, tail, side, and leg of an elephant and then define *elephant* in four different ways based on what they have perceived. The perspectives are about viewing clinical information and then, because the perspectives are plural, about communicating that information to clinicians, colleagues, and, most important, the individual with the clinical problem or disorder.

The perspectives were developed by Paul McHugh and Phillip Slavney, as the chairman and the director of residency training, respectively, in the Department of Psychiatry at the Johns Hopkins School of Medicine.(1) The perspectives methodology emerged from the historical context of late-twentieth-century psychiatry, in which biological psychiatry was on the rise and traditional psychoanalytic psychiatry had lost much of its century-long dominance. Each camp had little regard for the other. To further add to the contentiousness, the three principal mental health professional groups — psychiatry, psychology, and social work — were more often than not locked in guild wars, exacerbated by the decreasing mental health dollars. Managed care was perceived as, and in many cases was, imposing its own financially driven model of treatment. Mental health practitioners rightly felt embattled and more often than not circled the wagons of guild or theoretical tradition. A healthy discourse among differing opinions and viewpoints was a rare occurrence.

As educators primarily of future psychiatrists, but also of psychologists and social workers, McHugh and Slavney sought to provide an academic setting in which the current debilitating contention and theoretical isolation among mental health clinicians would be replaced by an environment in which constructive dialogue and creative debate would thrive. From a decade of teaching and reflecting on what made for effective learning in the clinical setting, the perspectives method emerged. The method provided and continues to provide a structured way of fostering discussion and permitting rational debate about clinical cases in which respect for different viewpoints is a given. The perspectives provide legitimating structure so that both the biological psychopharmacologist and the psychoanalytically trained analyst can creatively discuss the same clinical case.

The Perspectives of Psychiatry was first published in 1986; a second edition appeared in 1998. In these texts, McHugh and Slavney describe in full the method of the perspectives as applied to psychiatric disorders in general. Two books have applied the perspectives method to specific areas within the full range of disorders: Phillip Slavney's *Perspectives on "Hysteria"* and David Neubauer's *Understanding Sleeplessness.* (2,3) Even more recently, a third text has related the perspectives to the biopsychosocial model.(4) This current book, then, is the fourth application of the perspectives methodology—in this case, to the field of sexual disorders and sexual dysfunctions.

The chapters that follow treat in more detail the characteristics of each perspective as it is applied to sexual disorders. At this point, a general overview of the perspectives can provide a basic understanding of what the perspectives are and how they relate to important topics, among them the biopsychosocial model, psychiatric history and mental status examination, and formulation and diagnoses. This introductory chapter concludes with some specific features of the perspectives that the clinician should keep in mind as they are applied to sexual disorders throughout this book.

TABLE 1.1

An Overview of the Perspectives

Perspective	Logic	What the Patient ——	Treatment
Disease	Categories	Has.	Alleviate or cure
Dimension	Gradation and quantification	Is.	Assist in adaptation and response
Behavior	Goal directed, teleological	Does.	Interrupt, replace behaviors
Life story	Narrative	Encounters and gives meaning to.	Reinterpret or reconstruct narrative

Source: McHugh PR. Managed care and the four perspectives. Paper presented at Academic Behavioral Healthcare Consortium, June 15, 2001.

THE INTERNAL STRUCTURE OF THE FOUR PERSPECTIVES

The four perspectives are disease, dimension, behavior, and life story. Table 1.1 compares them in terms of their logic, relationship to the patient, and treatment goals.(5) Each perspective contributes to organizing the clinician's thinking about an individual who consults a mental health professional for evaluation and treatment. The result of employing the four perspectives is a formulation of the case that is comprehensive yet open to further information and even revision.

The Disease Perspective

The disease perspective's logic or way of thinking is categorical: the patient has the disease (category) or does not. A differential diagnosis contains a list of possible diseases or morbid conditions that the patient may have. The logic of disease is the ruling in or ruling out of each item of the differential diagnosis. The treatment goal of the disease perspective is to alleviate the pain or limitations of the disease or to cure it.

The disease perspective, of course, is the foundation of the medical model. Physicians are professionally trained in this model, and while nonphysicians can admit the clear logic and empiricism of the medical model of the disease perspective, they are typically more comfortable with the psychosocial aspects of a case and may have to labor intentionally to consistently give the disease perspective its due. But more about this later.

The Dimension Perspective

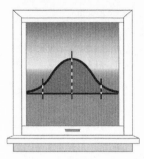

The most succinct way to describe the dimension perspective is to recall the work traditionally done by the psychologist in the psychological assessment of an individual. The assessment is a measurement (dimensional gradations and quantification) of an individual's functioning. Intelligence quotient (I.Q.), personality traits, and behavioral patterns are the objects of the measurement. To the extent that the function accurately reflects the abilities and potential of the one being assessed, then to that extent, but only to that extent, can we say that it measures what that person is. If an I.Q. of 125 is accurately measured, we can say that this person is above average in intelligence.

In terms of treatment, the dimension perspective is concerned with the relative strengths and vulnerabilities of the individual. These (e.g., I.Q. or other qualities or traits the person may have) are "relative" to a normative sample. Treatment goals are achieved by employing the strengths of the individual while helping to develop strategies to avoid the weaknesses or vulnerabilities. In doing this, the individual is adapting behaviors that are more responsive to the demands of his or her situation.

Clinicians who value such measurements and the contributions they make to the development of treatment plans will respond favorably to the dimension perspective's additive value to the formulation of a clinical case. Those who see quantification as a distraction from the understanding of the patient may tend to devalue the information provided by the dimension perspective.

The Behavior Perspective

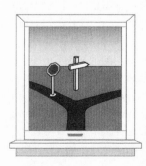

The behavior perspective is focused on the behavior of an individual that is goal directed, or teleological. Its logic says that an individual performs a specific behavior to achieve a certain end or consequence. Furthermore, the behavior perspective examines the antecedents that affect the expression of that behavior and the consequences that result from the behavior. When the consequences are beneficial to self and others, there is no need to break the antecedent → behavior → consequence sequence. When there are problems with the consequences —

the presence or absence of behaviors causes harm—the behavior perspective seeks remedy by interrupting or replacing the behaviors.

The behavior perspective is to cognitive-behavioral clinicians what the disease perspective is to physicians. For the former group, the behavior perspective entails the well-known and empirically supported treatment protocols for problematic behaviors. Clinicians who tend to avoid a behavioral focus in their treatments will find it a challenge to use the behavior perspective. But for those cases in which a behavior is clearly harmful to the patient or to others, even these clinicians welcome the contributions made by this perspective.

The Life Story Perspective

The life story perspective is what most people associate with psychotherapy. This perspective relies on the narrative told by the patient to give some meaning and direction to his or her life. The past events that have been formative in the course of a person's life—those that have either given meaning and purpose or called into question meaning and purpose—are woven into a narrative by the patient with the assistance of the therapist. Treatment in the life story perspective is indicated when the thread of the individual's life has begun to unravel and meaning is lost or is bent on a destructive path. The treatment then becomes the reinterpretation and reconstruction of a life narrative that will give meaning and direction to that person's life.

Clinicians whose work in psychotherapy naturally involves the personal history employ the life story perspective. Psychoanalytic, object relations, existential, Jungian, Adlerian—almost all developmental theories as applied to psychotherapy use the life story perspective. The challenge of using this perspective is to give it the proper value in each particular clinical case. The extremes need to be avoided: either relying exclusively on this perspective to provide all answers or dismissing it as relativistic and irrelevant to treatment needs.

EXTERNAL RELATIONSHIPS OF THE FOUR PERSPECTIVES

The Perspectives and Sexual Science

Despite the amount of information abroad about sex, we are only beginning to understand the multifactorial causes of sexual behavior, especially the interaction of biological effects and cultural contexts.(6)

Nowhere is this more apparent than in the shift in the causal attributions that have been applied to male sexual arousal in the past twenty-five years. Until the mid-1970s, a combination of the life story and behavior perspectives was used to explain erectile dysfunction in the vast majority of cases. Only those men who had obvious neurological and/or vascular diseases were thought to have "organic" causes of erectile dysfunction. All other men with erectile dysfunction had "performance anxiety" or "spectatoring" (behavior perspective), or the sexual dysfunction was an expression of some unresolved conflict arising earlier in life (life story perspective).

Enter, in the early 1990s, the disease perspective, with its interest in physiological function in sexual arousal. Basic research on nitric oxide's effect on penile arousal was applied by Pfizer Pharmaceuticals, which produced and marketed sildenafil, Viagra.(7) With the advent of the oral medication in 1998, many speculated that there would no longer be a need for a psychological approach to erectile dysfunction: the pill would solve everything. Erectile dysfunction was to be considered a medical disorder and treated with medical interventions. The disease perspective had nearly replaced the behavior and life story perspectives as the operative perspective on male erectile dysfunction.

Other clinicians did not remain silent about what appeared to them as a reductionistic reliance on the medical/disease perspective. Social constructionism theorists, researchers, and experienced sexual clinicians, writing and speaking largely from the life story perspective, challenged the rise of the medicalization of sexuality (the disease perspective).(8,9) Their argument was that human sexuality is a far more complex reality than the achievement of reliable erections. They pressed for the inclusion of psychological and relational factors distinct from physiological function when researchers wanted to report on the efficacy of a treatment for sexual disorders. Although these theorists did not intend to employ a four-perspectives methodology, they did in fact work with this method. They took a prevailing perspective and brought other perspectives into dialogue with it.

The four perspectives, each through its relativity to the others, offer checks and balances to the reductionism that may result from the application of a single perspective. There is a constant "but what about . . . ?" refrain that requires the sexual scientist and clinician to consider something they may have overlooked or prematurely dismissed. In all areas of psychiatric thought — but perhaps most in sexual behavior, with its biological, psychological, and cultural components — the four perspectives provide an open-ended dynamic for looking at cases and problems with new questions.

The Perspectives and the Biopsychosocial Model

At first glance, the perspectives methodology may seem to be Adolf Meyer's psychobiology revisited.(10) As later developed by George Engel, the biopsychosocial model urges clinicians, in treating their patients, to take into account aspects of biology, psychology, and culture.(11,12) In recent years, the model has been of special interest in the treatment of psychosomatic conditions such as chronic pain, where it has proved effective.(13,14) In psychiatry there has been a renewed call for research on the integration of pharmacotherapy and psychotherapy in the name of biopsychosocial integration.(15)

What, then, is the relationship of the perspectives model to the biopsychosocial model? Simply put, the perspectives provide a method of using the central insight of the biopsychosocial model: that there are multiple determinants of behaviors and conditions arising from biology, psychology, and the social and physical environment. Because nothing a priori is excluded in the biopsychosocial model, its application can pose a heuristic challenge. Recall that Engel's levels of organization in his systems hierarchy spanned everything from subatomic particles to the biosphere. Granted, no clinician or researcher attempts to consider and control for the universe of possible factors; nevertheless, methodological assistance is needed to decide how to go about considering the literally "too numerous to number" factors that make up our biopsychosocial world.

Enter the perspectives methodology. The perspectives take on the challenge of the biopsychosocial approach to consider nearly everything in the formulation of the individual case and to organize the data into four major perspectives. Employed diligently, these organizing perspectives assist the clinician to consider, if not "everything" in the biopsychosocial universe, at least a great deal more than he or she might consider without the methodology. In addition, the repeated interaction of the perspectives assists the clinician to link together the various strata of the biopsychosocial model in an effective treatment approach.

In the most recent description of his perspectives, Paul McHugh places "the perspectives into a view of human mental life as organized hierarchically into four distinct but interrelated domains from the most neurologically basic to the most individually highly developed."(16) Table 1.2 is McHugh's scheme of how the perspectives relate to each

TABLE 1.2

Hierarchical Levels of Human Mental Life:
Their Disorders and Treatment

Perspective	Components of Psychological Life	Modes of Mental Disorder	Treatment Initiatives
Life story	Personal chronicle	Disruptive life stories	Reframe
Dimension	Constitutional dimensions	Problematic dispositions	Guide
Behavior	Motivational rhythms	Behavior disorders	Interrupt
Disease	Cerebral faculties	Psychiatric diseases	Remedy

other in the biopsychosocial world and, even more, how they address modes of mental disorders and basic treatment goals. Each of these components interacts with the others; the table expresses how the perspectives are structured from the most basic neurological level to the most complex cognitive one.

Clearly, then, the perspectives methodology is not antithetical to the biopsychosocial model. In addition to the organizing function, at least three of the four perspectives — disease, behavior, and life story perspectives — assume there are biological and psychosocial components in the genesis and treatment of psychiatric disorders. The remaining perspective, dimension, seeks to measure constructs that are biological, cultural, and psychological. In that sense, the perspectives are built on and employ the biopsychosocial model.

The perspectives thus are a methodological supplement to the biopsychosocial model, because they help organize and apply the latter model in the individual cases presented to a mental health clinician. If the biopsychosocial model is a unified theory that seeks to explain all causes, the perspectives are much more modest in their aim. The perspectives model suggests the methods one might employ to put the biopsychosocial model into rational practice. In many ways, the perspectives are the operational testing and application of biopsychosocial theory.

The perspectives help one to avoid using a ritualized invocation of the biopsychosocial model and then proceeding with a treatment regimen that ignores key elements. A recent survey of 54 (of 118 polled) U.S. medical schools suggested that while many attempts are made to teach biopsychosocial medicine to future physicians, there are generally still barriers in the development of a unified curriculum that might be described as "biopsychosocial."(17) This survey of medical schools is probably a good indication of most treatment approaches today: the biopsy-chosocial is invoked as the model guiding evaluation and treatment, but barriers remain to its being as influential as it might be. The perspectives are an attempt to provide a way of increasing the effectiveness of the biopsychosocial model.

Just as with the biopsychosocial model, it is not a question of "new" knowledge in employing the perspectives. Every aspect of the perspectives has already been written about and employed clinically. It would be erroneous, therefore, to expect some new information from the perspectives themselves. What is original is the structured organization of the perspectives. The essence of the working of the perspectives is dialectical. They take the clinician's "I know such and such" and invite him or her to hear, "But you must also consider your patient from this other perspective." Then, from the application of the newly adopted perspectives, the clinician achieves a fuller appreciation of the disorder and approaches for treating the disorder.

The Perspectives, Psychiatric History, and Mental Status Examination

The perspectives methodology requires a certain body of information and data about an individual before it can be fully used. This basic level of knowledge is usually obtained in the initial evaluation, together with psychological assessment and interviews with available patient informants (e.g., family members). The evaluation of the patient consists of a full psychiatric history and mental status examination. These two procedures, in particular, provide information about possible familial predispositions for disorders, key developmental data, personal psychiatric history, history of substance use, and a behavioral assessment of present mental and emotional functioning.

The history and mental status examination have traditionally been the domain of psychiatry, although more and more social workers and psychologists, especially those associated with mental health facilities, now take initial histories and conduct mental status examinations. Indeed, it is the responsibility of the mental health evaluator, regardless of professional group, to provide the information garnered in the history and mental status examination. If the clinician does not obtain a full history and mental status examination in the initial stage of therapy, but rather proceeds without this knowledge to "let the history unfold," it is nearly impossible to see how the full perspectives methodology could be employed. The clinician seems to have opted for the life story perspective,

while information vital for the other perspectives depends on a fortu-
itous unfolding of the history.

The Perspectives, Clinical Formulation, and DSM-IV-TR Diagnoses

A psychological or psychiatric evaluation consists of the history, mental
status examination, and data provided by psychological assessment and
informants. The goal of the evaluation is to construct a formulation of
the case — the clinician's summary of the complex interaction of factors
that may have influenced the form, content, and function of the disorder that brings the individual into treatment. It is the product, clearly,
of the skill and clinical wisdom of the evaluating mental health professional.

The diagnosis is one element of the formulation that relates the clinical presentation of the particular patient to the larger world of clinical
syndromes, disorders, and problematic behaviors. The *Diagnostic and
Statistical Manual of Mental Disorders-IV-TR*(18) and the entire DSM
series have been an effort to provide empirically valid and reliable criteria for psychiatric diagnostic categories. One of the most remarkable
achievements of North American psychiatry, the DSM has facilitated research and reliable communication in the mental health field by organizing symptoms and behaviors into psychiatric diagnoses.

Two extremes are found among mental health practitioners' attitudes
toward DSM-IV-TR diagnoses. In one camp are those who believe their
sole evaluation task is to assign the proper diagnosis according to DSM-
IV-TR criteria. For these clinicians, determining the proper diagnosis is
the goal of the evaluation. Following the intention of the DSM-IV-TR,
in reaching a diagnosis they are driven not by theory but by their empirical findings in the patient's history and mental status examination.
Clinical research protocols often are concerned only with diagnosis, because of their interest in study participants that meet the symptom-
inclusion profile.

In the other camp are mental health clinicians who are quite indiffer-
ent to DSM diagnoses and avoid them at all possible costs — excluding
requests from third-party payers, of course. This group is more interested in letting the patient's history unfold in the course of therapy. They
tend to see diagnostic categories as unfortunate limitations to the complexity of the person's psychological history and status. For these clinicians, the formulation of the case is a process constantly open to revision
based on new information provided in the course of psychotherapy.

The perspectives methodology assists in both the diagnosis and the formulation of the individual case. After obtaining a full history and mental status examination from the patient, the clinician who employs the perspectives methodology will be able to provide the objective and empirical data required by the DSM-IV-TR while also having garnered sufficient information to develop a rich formulation of the person and the disorder. Diagnosis is not sufficient for clinical treatment in psychiatric disorders or in sexual disorders. More must be said about a case than diagnosis, and this "more" is information that is organized with the perspectives methodology.

NOTES ON EMPLOYING THE FOUR PERSPECTIVES

First among Equals

No single perspective is, in itself, more valuable than any other. However, in a particular case, some perspectives are more salient than others. For example, the case of a 25-year-old woman presenting with florid manic behaviors would primarily be formulated using the disease perspective. She has bipolar illness and requires, perhaps among other treatments, medication for the regulation of her central nervous system (CNS) neurotransmitters. Or, consider a recently widowed 79-year-old woman. Most persons who sustain the loss of a loved one must work to restore some meaning to their lives; the life story perspective is most salient here. An alcoholic man who wishes to stop drinking is best understood and assisted with the behavior perspective. Last, the case of a shy and introverted man who has been promoted into a situation that demands public leadership is formulated most easily with the dimension perspective.

All Perspectives Can Contribute

Mentioning these four different examples, however, does not mean there is a simple one-to-one application of a perspective to a case. Each perspective can contribute to the formulation. The young woman with manic symptoms and bipolar disorder may also have a drinking problem, and so the behavior perspective will be employed in the treatment once the manic symptoms have been controlled. The widow may not be able to shake her grief after one year, and she not only becomes demoralized but also has a major depressive disorder. At this point, the disease perspective, with its recommendations of antidepressant medication, will complement the life story treatment that has been primary thus far. The alcoholic who is able to remain sober for several months may for the first time start asking questions about the meaning of relationships and work in his life. Treatment in the life story perspective will assist his understanding of the past and, more important, construct goals and directions toward those goals. The shy and introverted manager may well compensate his personality vulnerabilities with coaching and self-development programs in public speaking. This is the contribution of the behavior perspective.

Continuous Review Is Required

The mental health clinician who takes the four perspectives seriously will perform a "perspectives review" of each new patient and, with current patients, at regular intervals in the ongoing treatment. Simply put, for any case, a perspectives review applies the discipline of each perspective anew and constructs a revised formulation according to what one learns. This practice has two immediate effects: (i) it fosters collegial consultation and referral, and (ii) it assists the clinician to avoid the myopic practice of treating all patients with the same treatment approach, simply because that is what he or she knows.

Clinicians using the four perspectives do not use the single arrow in the quiver of treatment methods but rather expand their knowledge of the perspectives by education and training. If needs be, they are willing to refer the patient to a colleague who can address his or her needs with a more salient perspective, one that they do not have the ability to employ. Most clinicians are skilled in formulating and treating their patients with two perspectives. Some might be above average in three perspectives. Rarely is someone an expert in all four perspectives. Therefore, the clinician seeks collegial guidance, supervision, and referral. Openness to the four perspectives works against a faddish, if not cultist, following of the newest treatment method. Rather, the clinician is prompted to develop an internal openness to the other perspectives and a relational openness to consultation with colleagues.

THE PERSPECTIVES AND SEXUAL DISORDERS

Even as the perspectives are an effective epistemology in the formulation of cases of general psychiatric disorders, so too do they provide clinicians with a comprehensive approach to individuals with sexual disorders and dysfunctions. After all, sexual disorders and sexual dysfunction are conditions, behaviors, and problems that are usually diagnosable with DSM-IV-TR criteria. What I have said about the perspectives and psychiatric disorders in general applies equally to sexual disorders.

The perspectives assist clinicians to organize information about sexual behaviors and sexual disorders. Across the various professions and disciplines, the main challenge today is not a dearth of information but how to manage and organize the torrent of information available from sources such as the Internet into knowledge that is personally and professionally useful. The added challenge of sexual information is its multidisciplinary origins: physiology, medicine, anthropology, sociology, and psychology. The perspectives provide a discipline that aids the clinician to organize the data coming from these varied sources as he or she attempts to evaluate and treat a sexual disorder.

1. The *disease perspective* turns to physiology, anatomy, and medicine and asks what can be learned about the patient's sexual problem from these disciplines. For example, is the low sexual desire caused by abnormally low testosterone?
2. The *dimension perspective* employs the results gained from an evaluation of the individual's personality or intelligence to assess his or her abilities to meet the conditions resulting from current sexual problems or challenges. For example, is a shy and introverted man plummeted into performance anxiety as he attempts to initiate sex with his partner?
3. The *behavior perspective* helps both the clinician and the patient with a problematic sexual behavior to focus on the behavior rather than collude in addressing more remote issues that are perhaps less anxiety provoking for therapist and patient. Take, for example, the individual who has sexually assaulted children and was sexually assaulted himself as a child. The therapy and life task is to control his pedophilic urges, not to dwell on the trauma suffered decades ago.
4. The *life story perspective* states that meaning is important and that sexual behaviors are not universal in their perceived meaning. Meaning-bearing institutions (e.g., religion, academia, developmental psychology, as well as the cultural myths gained from anthropology) are important in the life story perspective as they pertain to sexual expression and behaviors.

SEX: FORM, CONTENT, AND FUNCTION

One of the introductory sections in *The Perspectives of Psychiatry* discusses the constructs of *form, content,* and *function.* There are applications here to sexual disorders, so some brief comments are in order about these constructs, drawing, as an example, from the movie *A Beautiful Mind.* In the movie, Nobel Prize winner John Nash, a man with paranoid schizophrenia, experiences visual hallucinations of a college roommate, the roommate's young niece, and an intricate web of Department of Defense activity to ward off the threat of the Russians detonating a nuclear device in the United States during the 1950s.

It is helpful to distinguish among form, content, and function to understand psychiatrically what is being presented in the movie. The form is the mental activity that is occurring, the visual and auditory hallucinations: John Nash sees and hears individuals who do not exist. The content is what the hallucinations are about, what is "seen and heard": the roommate, the niece, and the multiple players in the Department of Defense–Russian drama. The function is what purpose these phenomena might play in John Nash's psychological life: hypothetically, fulfilling a need to be recognized as a genius.

Much of the debate, confusion, and lack of appropriate treatment in the history of twentieth-century psychiatry lay in clinicians not making the distinctions among form, content, and function. All too often, only one of the three was made the object of treatment. Especially harmful to generations of patients was psychiatry's overlooking the form of the mental activity. Psychotic activity was "therapeutically mined" for meaningful connections to the unconscious conflicts within the patient. The psychotic process was, in practice, ignored. In some mental hospitals, antipsychotic medications were considered inappropriate because they would interfere with the meaning (function) of the hallucinations or delusions. To lose access to the hallucinations would be to lose access to the unconscious in psychotherapy. Function and content not only trumped form but also rendered it an unconsidered construct.

Form, content, and function are no less important when considering sexual dysfunctions and disorders. The clinician should have a clear idea of each and be able to draw the necessary distinctions among the constructs. It is useful to consider a case story here.

■ Michael was a 45-year-old teacher. He was sexually attracted to prepubescent boys and had acted on the attraction on multiple occasions. He was Roman Catholic and felt very guilty about the repeated behaviors. Michael had attempted to have a sexual relationship with both adult men and women but was sexually attracted to neither.

The *form* of the behavior described here is ego-dystonic homosexual pedophilia that is exclusive. Michael was ambivalent about the behavior and, at least partly, wished that it were not in his life. He was sexually attracted to prepubescent individuals of his own gender. Any other type of individual could not sexually arouse him. The form of the behavior usually provides information useful in meeting the diagnostic criteria of the DSM-IV-TR.

The *content* of the behavior is the myriad of details in the relationships and incidents involved in the pedophilic activity. Who were the victims? What were their relationships to Michael? What type of seduction did he employ? What went through his mind before, during, and after the pedophilic activity?

The *function* of the behavior is the purpose attributed to the pedophilic behavior in Michael's life. It is the meaning he attached to the behavior and/or the meaning hypothesized by his therapist as motivating Michael to continue the behavior. Examples of function for Michael might be (i) to compensate for a childhood bereft of male affection, because his father abandoned the family when Michael was 2 years old; (ii) to assuage his poor sense of self as an effective male by exercising power over young males; or (iii) to obtain sexual release with the most convenient and attractive persons available to him. Function is a hypothesis that is tested in the therapeutic process for subjective validation from the patient as he or she attempts to consider the function in a critical manner.

The perspectives methodology is a strategy to preserve the practical distinction among the constructs of form, content, and function. Function is clear in the life story perspective, while the other three perspectives address form and function separately.

As each of these perspectives is described in the following chapters, it will become apparent that the perspectives do not so much add to what is presently done by clinicians as organize and help ensure that the formulation and treatment of sexual disorders are as comprehensive as possible for the clinical case.

SEXUAL DIAGNOSES

Given that the sexual diagnosis must be the product of a full formulation of the case before beginning treatment, I note here some special features of sexual diagnoses in particular. While these diagnoses share the DSM structure, with its aim of empirically verifiable and replicable criteria, some qualities in sexual behaviors and problems warrant comment.

Not All Sexually Disordered Behavior Has a Psychiatric Diagnosis

Many problematic sexual behaviors are not currently considered psychiatric disorders. Rape and sexual aggression are examples. Rapists are a heterogeneous group, and some commit rape not because it is the preferred sexual expression and therefore paraphilic but because of other factors (e.g., antisocial personality).(19) Unwelcome sexual contact or sexual aggressiveness has been reported by more than 50 percent of women,(20) a prevalence that argues more for cultural factors (interactions between genders) than for paraphilic disorders in males. Using the Internet access at the workplace for erotic exchanges and sexual release may show extremely poor impulse control, poor judgment, and deficient employee integrity, but it may not be a sexual disorder. Sexual harassment and multiple extramarital affairs may cause loss of employment and divorce, but they are not necessarily sexual disorders. If we were, then, to limit our discussion of sexual disorders to those thus classified by the DSM-IV-TR, we would be omitting many of the pressing sexual questions of the day.

This is not a plea to pathologize such behaviors and give them a DSM-IV-TR diagnosis. It is a recognition that many problematic sexual behaviors are brought to the attention of mental health clinicians with the request that they assist in correcting or stopping them. These behaviors require a means of formulation that is adequate to hypothesize about the probable causative influences and maintaining factors and to propose treatments. The perspectives methodology guides the clinician and treatment team in this process by structuring their use of established approaches and stretching their thinking to consider yet other perspectives.

Sexual Diagnosis Does Not Imply Causality

The explicit aim of the DSM series is to avoid in its criteria any assumptions about the causality of the sexual diagnoses. Thus, for example, Inhibited Sexual Desire (DSM-III) was changed to Hypoactive Sexual Desire in DSM-III-R. The editors rightly felt that the word *inhibited* implied a causal factor. Accordingly, the editors of DSM-III-R changed *inhibited* to *hypoactive,* on the grounds that this term is more descriptive without any etiological bias. Persons with the diagnosis Hypoactive Sexual Desire may or may not be inhibited by biological, psychological, or cultural factors. To make this distinction or to imply this influence in the disorder is not the function of the diagnostic category.

The clinician employing the perspectives as a methodology to guide thinking about sexual disorders is interested in the genesis, course, and treatment of sexual disorders. The perspectives certainly assist in establishing diagnoses, by describing the cluster of symptoms and quantifying the behaviors evident in the individual patient. Responding to the question of etiology, the clinician using the perspectives methodology strives to avoid ascribing to one factor the entire causal variance. If there is a bias in the perspectives, it is one of assuming multifactorial causality. For those who want "single cause, single solution" according to diagnosis protocols, the perspectives will seem to unnecessarily complicate a simple process. For those who use a perspectives methodology, the categorical diagnosis is the result of a complex review of clinical data and impressions from several approaches.

Sexual Diagnosis Is an Alterable Construct

Diagnoses have changed and will continue to change in terms of their criteria. New diagnoses will be developed—though, it is to be hoped, only after they have been justified as a distinct clinical entity in research. DSM-IV-TR diagnoses, therefore, cannot be the final word on the phenomenology of disorders. Diagnoses are certainly helpful, as noted previously, but they should not be counted on for the ultimate statement about a condition.

In sexual function research, many are dissatisfied with the application of the human sexual response cycle as the basis for sexual dysfunction in women. Rosemary Basson developed a theoretical model of female sexual response,(21) and Ellen Laan and colleagues offered experimental research support for the model.(22) The Basson model basically says that the sequential desire-arousal-orgasm-resolution model that has been fairly normative for the past forty years does not fit the arousal patterns of women, especially those in long-term relationships who may not have spontaneous thoughts about sex but may be quite able to respond sexually to their partners out of a desire for intimacy. Laan's research supports the centrality of the arousal function in women and that the woman's subjective sense of sexual arousal is often not correlated with vaginal lubrication and swelling.

The point of mentioning the Basson and Laan works is to note that sexual diagnoses are alterable constructs. Yet clinicians and researchers must continue to use the present diagnostic nomenclature while at the same time marshalling theoretical arguments and data for the alteration or abandonment of specific diagnoses. This requires a breadth of vision that can coordinate information from many quarters. It requires an ability to listen to those whose paradigms of organizing data are quite diverse. Clinician and researcher alike are stretched to consider data and constructs from different perspectives. It is helpful to have a methodology that enables one to consider and eventually integrate the different perspectives. Some would say that it is more than helpful — it is imperative. In this latter spirit, the perspectives are presented here for the reader's consideration.

SUMMARY

The perspectives are a methodology for organizing one's thinking about the problems that patients bring to mental health clinicians. Two decades ago, McHugh and Slavney developed the perspectives methodology to assist psychiatry residents in developing their diagnostic and treatment skills as they provided services to their patients. The perspectives — disease, dimension, behavior, and life story — also have applicability to clinical treatment of persons with sexual disorders and dysfunctions. Building on the general principles of the biopsychosocial model, the perspectives methodology enables the clinician to organize the abundance of information about the clinical problems of sexuality and develop a full formulation of the case. The formulation includes diagnoses, but it further suggests an understanding of the disorder's origins and recommends treatment. The perspectives methodology is especially helpful for sexual problems and disorders because these are among the most complex cases a clinician encounters. Sexual disorders and problems, of their very nature, involve biology, psychology, interpersonal relationships, and values and norms of the cultural milieu. How to organize and evaluate data emerging from these often competing domains is the challenge that the perspectives methodology can help the clinician meet. The following chapters present an exposition of how the mental health clinician can employ the perspectives in the treatment of sexual disorders and dysfunctions.

■ 2

SEX AND THE
DISEASE PERSPECTIVE

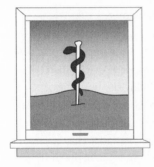

Sex involves the body. When the body is diseased, is injured by accident or surgery, or simply ages, there can be profound effects on the sexual life of the individual. Frequently, the clinician and the patient alike overlook the somatic conditions necessary for full sexual functioning and instead give a psychological interpretation of the cause of the dysfunction. Although it may seem obvious, one must listen to the body, its complaints, and its vulnerabilities when attempting to comprehend a sexual disorder and to design a treatment plan.

The body is involved in all sexual expression. Sexual desire arises from the viscera, is expressed through torso and limbs, is perceived through all five senses, and last — and if all goes well — quietly leaves a spent body. The Romans said, "Post coitum, omne animal triste est" (after sex, every animal is sad). "Sad" may be a poor translation of *triste*. Perhaps a better translation would be a combination of "spent, relaxed, satiated, and, in some instances, misty." While there are certainly emotional qualities to postcoital *triste*, it reminds us also of the somatic nature of sex. Sexual expression is a bodily reality. If something goes afoul with the body, the implications can be profound. For sexual expression to be its somatic fullest, the four horsemen of disease, disability, drugs, and aging must to a certain extent be kept at bay. When any one of them holds sway, the *triste* of sexual expression may precede rather than follow the act.

TABLE 2.1

An Overview of the Disease Perspective in the Context
of the Other Three Perspectives

Perspective	Logic	What the Patient _____	Treatment
Disease	**Categories**	**Has.**	**Alleviate or cure**
Dimension	Gradation and quantification	Is.	Assist in adaptation and response
Behavior	Goal directed, teleological	Does.	Interrupt, replace behaviors
Life story	Narrative	Encounters and gives meaning to.	Reinterpret or reconstruct narrative

Source: McHugh PR. Managed care and the four perspectives. Paper presented at Academic Behavioral Healthcare Consortium, June 15, 2001.

AN OVERVIEW OF THE DISEASE PERSPECTIVE

The logic of the disease perspective is, strictly speaking, categorical (see Table 2.1). Its goal is to group conditions into diagnostic categories based on the pathological conditions found in individuals. Ultimately, the disease perspective seeks to state whether a person has — or does not have — a particular disease. Does this person have tuberculosis, yes or no?

To make this determination, the reasoning of the disease perspective follows three stages: (i) it identifies the symptoms; (ii) it links the symptoms to some abnormal body structure or function; and (iii) it determines the underlying cause of the pathological process. McHugh describes these three steps as the conceptual triad that organizes the disease perspective: clinical entity, pathological condition, and etiology.(1)

The *clinical entity* is the cluster of signs and symptoms present in the individual. Identifying clinical entities is the empirical work of observing and noting phenomena. In the mental status examination, for example, attention is given to the manner of dress, speech rate and rhythm, bodily movements, and any other physical quality or behavior.

■ Frank consulted the clinician for an evaluation of his premature ejaculation. His marriage of twelve years was stable, and the premature ejaculation had developed over the past six months. During the evaluation, he sweated profusely and seemed to be physically agitated. He was referred for a long-overdue physical examination and was found to have hyperthyroidism. As the thyroid function was normalized with medication, the premature ejaculation resolved.

Certainly, no clinician would diagnose hyperthyroidism based on sweating and agitation alone. But attention to these clinical entities should alert one to the need for further physical and laboratory evaluation in a patient who has not recently had a complete medical examination.

The *pathological condition* is the abnormal somatic function or diseased organ that is linked to the cluster of observed symptoms. For Frank, the excessive secretion of thyroid hormone was the pathological condition. The hyperactive thyroid produced his sweating, agitation, and premature ejaculation and also produced poor sleep and weight loss despite an increased appetite. The pathological condition was linked with these symptoms or clinical entities through laboratory studies of his thyroid function.

The *etiology* is the causative factor — not the hyperthyroidism, which is the pathological condition, but what is causing the hyperthyroidism. Unfortunately, the exact cause of Frank's hyperthyroidism was unknown. Although many causes of diseases can be identified (e.g., *Mycobacterium tuberculosis* causes tuberculosis), unknown causality is not uncommon. Indeed, finding etiological factors is the ongoing work of medical research. Until the causes are found, clinical medicine is limited to treating the symptoms. Fortunately for Frank and for others with thyroid diseases, medication can greatly reduce the symptoms and allow normal functioning.

Application of the disease perspective to sexual disorders is the work of ensuring that the somatic factors, disease processes, and physiological functions, as they may relate to the cause or expression of the sexual disorder or dysfunction, have been identified. It entails linking the clinical entities with a pathological condition. In sexual problems, the clinical entities of the sexual dysfunction and the patient's medical history may indicate the pathological condition. The linking of the two is the task of the disease perspective. Table 2.2 lists some common linkages between sexual problems (clinical entities) and medical illnesses (pathological conditions).

Treatment in the disease perspective is to cure the disease or, when that is not possible, to alleviate the symptoms. When sexual dysfunction is present as a helpful sign or symptom (clinical entity) of an underlying pathological condition, treatment is given to address the pathological condition. When one cannot successfully treat the underlying condition (e.g., peripheral neuropathy), symptomatic treatment is given (e.g., oral medication for erectile function). Another clinical case can illustrate the work of the disease perspective.

TABLE 2.2

Linkages between Sexual Clinical Entities and the
Pathological Conditions Responsible

Sexual Problem — Clinical Entity	Pathological Condition Probably Causing Sexual Problem
Hypoactive sexual desire	Any chronic systemic disease
Hypoactive desire and arousal	Multiple sclerosis; major depression
Hypoactive arousal and orgasm	Alcoholic neuropathy
Painful intercourse	Endometriosis; atrophic vaginitis

■ Ralph was a 45-year-old man who had enjoyed a twenty-year marriage with his wife. Their three children, now in their teens, added no more than the usual amount of *Sturm und Drang* of adolescence to the household. Ralph had been in sales throughout his career and presently was making another shift in employment — this time to assume major responsibility for a national product line.

Ralph was in apparent good health, although slightly overweight. He drank one beer daily with his main meal and exercised infrequently. In their sexual life, Ralph and his wife had usually had intercourse about three times a month and neither had experienced sexual dysfunction — until recently.

For the past several months, Ralph had noticed himself becoming less and less interested in sex. The frequency of intercourse had decreased, and he had not wanted to have sex for the past two months. Sexual thoughts and fantasies were absent. While he had masturbated on occasion in the past, this behavior was absent in the past six months. He noticed that he and his wife were not getting along as well as usual, and more frequently than in the past were "getting on each other's nerves."

Ralph consulted his physician, who ordered a serum testosterone level and liver function tests on the suspicion that Ralph had underreported the amount of his drinking and, in fact, may have reduced testosterone due to his alcohol consumption. The physician also assessed Ralph for depression. Other than being upset by his low libido, Ralph gave no indication of being clinically depressed. Even the strain of the transition to the new position at work was evoking in Ralph his typical "can do" optimism.

The serum testosterone level came back remarkably low. This explained the low sexual desire. But more remarkably, the pituitary (prolactin) level, measured at the same time, was correspondingly elevated. Ralph's physician suggested that he have an MRI to check for any lesion on his pituitary gland that might be causing the hyperprolactinemia.

The MRI reading came back positive. Ralph had a pituitary adenoma, a nonmalignant neoplasm on his pituitary gland. He began a regimen of bromocriptine. After several months' treatment, his levels of prolactin and testosterone had returned to normal. With the return of normal levels, Ralph regained his premorbid baseline of intercourse once a week.

Two years later, Ralph and his wife are back to enjoying sex at a frequency of about once every ten days; he has again switched to another company; and only one of the three children has gotten into academic trouble. In short, things are back to normal.

The disease perspective is the perspective most often used by physicians. For this reason, application of the disease reasoning process to psychiatric or behavioral disorders is often referred to, disparagingly, as the "medicalization" of psychological problems. Is this a fair critique?

If, in fact, the disease perspective is the only reasoning method in the mental health clinician's armamentarium, then his or her diagnostic reasoning will be reductionistic. But attempting to understand all problems as ultimately rooted in a bodily disease is not the disease perspective's rationale. As I will repeat often in this book, a particular perspective — in this case, the disease perspective — is but one way to understand and sometimes even causally explain a disorder. Ralph's case is a good example of this.

Ralph's low libido was the symptom that disturbed him (and his wife) and alerted the physician. He clearly was not as interested in either thinking about or having sex as he had previously been. While Ralph's low desire might have been attributed to a combination of aging, alcohol consumption, pressure at work, and tension at home, his physician ordered the proper tests. The low serum testosterone was the abnormal hormonal function responsible for his reduced sexual desire.

The physician then sought to explain why the testosterone level was so low. He discovered that high prolactin levels, hyperprolactinemia, were suppressing it. But what was the underlying cause of the high prolactin? The MRI indicated that a small, benign tumor — an adenoma — was growing on Ralph's pituitary gland, located deep within the subcortical area of his brain. Fortunately, surgery was not indicated and Ralph responded well to the oral medication.

If the disease perspective had not been employed here as the primary diagnostic and treatment perspective, then an expenditure of many months and dollars, and perhaps a further deterioration of the relationship between Ralph and his wife, might have followed. Hours of sexual or marriage counseling might have been spent on asking how much did Ralph really drink, were husband and wife taking each other for granted and not communicating well, was Ralph too involved in his work? While all these questions might be worthy of attention, it would have been a major therapeutic error to think that addressing them and attempting to make changes in these areas could have any substantial effect on Ralph's sexual desire. In addition to low libido, therapy-induced frustration would have been added to the symptom cluster.

A PSYCHIATRIC DISEASE

It is not always easy to see the connection between a sexual behavioral pattern and a disease process. Often this is because we notice the behaviors as a syndrome and correlate them with a psychiatric disorder that is not yet proven to have a pathological process in the body (brain). The case of Sally is helpful here.

■ Sally was a 43-year-old married woman whose husband was employed as a utility repairman. It was the second marriage for him and the third marriage for her. Together they had no children, but she had two daughters (ages 20 and 18) and he had a son (age 14) by previous marriages. She worked as a clerical staff person in a construction company.

They sought marriage counseling in crisis because Sally had had a sexual relationship with a neighbor, the father of one of her stepson's friends. In the initial history, Sally reported that she had always felt she had a higher sexual drive than other women she knew. She judged herself to be slightly better than average in appearance, and she thought she often "gave off vibes" to men that she was sexually interested in them, even though they had met only casually. She said that men usually responded to her, and it was not difficult to conclude a casual meeting with a sexual encounter. Sally judged that she had had approximately thirty to thirty-five sexual partners in her life, all of them men, except once when she engaged in a ménage à trois with a man and a woman.

Sally described most of the sex as involving little knowledge of the other person but very intense in terms of sexual drive and pleasure.

She felt that the men were interested in sex also and that neither they nor she sought any lasting or committed relationship. She said she loved her husband and did not want the recent sexual wandering to ruin the marriage as it had in the two previous marriages. She wanted this time to be different and was convinced that it would be.

In her initial history-taking session with Sally, Dr. M. took a complete and careful sexual history and a detailed mental status examination. From both the history and the present mental status, Dr. M. concluded that Sally's episodic high drive correlated with other symptoms of a bipolar II disorder.

On closer examination of the sexual encounters, Sally was able to see that there was an episodic quality in the frequency of the behaviors. For months she would have what she felt was low (for her) sexual desire and interest, and then a period ranging from four to six weeks when she would become, in her words, "sexually alive." Also during these periods of being sexually alive, Sally would have a great deal of energy, undertaking exercise programs, requiring little sleep because of all she wanted to accomplish, and, on occasion, spending to such a degree that she "maxed out" her three credit cards. During these periods, she felt as if she got along very well with her husband, although the spending caused arguments.

Sally could not describe her mood and energy level during the times between these periods of elevated mood and energy. The best she could do was to say, "It's kinda like I feel now, since the discovery of my sexual time with N." In the mental status examination of her present mood, Sally reported that she felt tired and was not sleeping well — which she attributed to her worries that the marriage might be breaking up. She had lost eight pounds in the past month and wanted sex with her husband only to help keep the marriage going, not because of any sexual desire or interest on her part. While she felt somewhat guilty about the sex with her neighbor, it was difficult for her to distinguish the guilt about the behavior itself from the deep regret that the trysts were discovered and her marriage threatened.

Dr. M. learned other facts about Sally that confirmed her diagnosis of bipolar II disorder. Although Sally had never received treatment from a psychiatrist or other mental health provider, her mother had been hospitalized on three occasions. The first time occurred in her mother's early twenties and the diagnosis was schizophrenia. The last two hospitalizations had occurred within the past twenty years, and her mother was diagnosed with bipolar disorder and alcohol abuse. For the past seven years her mother had done well, avoiding alcohol and being maintained on a regimen of lithium carbonate and, more recently, Depakote (valproic acid) to keep her mood stable.

With the familial factor of affective illness, and the carefully obtained psychiatric history, Dr. M. concluded that Sally's sexual behaviors were caused, in large part, by her affective illness. The bipolar II disorder increased her libido and diminished her ability to judge the appropriateness of her behaviors, both sexual and financial. At the time of her sexual escapades, Sally clearly had only a vague awareness of the consequences that her behaviors might have on her life and on the relationships she valued.

Dr. M. recommended both psychopharmacological and psychotherapeutic treatment. Because Sally's mother responded well to Depakote, Dr. M. started Sally on that medication, in addition to a serotonin-specific antidepressant for her present depression. The psychotherapy had two goals: to understand Sally's vulnerability to the excesses of bipolar disorder and to "make some sense" of the prolific sexual experiences she had had in her life.

Psychiatric disorders such as bipolar disorder, major depressive disorder, and schizophrenia are as much the result of disease processes as are somatic diseases such as pituitary adenoma or tuberculosis. As such, they deserve the same diagnostic strategies and consideration of appropriate somatic treatments (e.g., medication). Most of these psychiatric diseases affect a patient's sexual functioning.

In the initial diagnostic stage of treatment, the disease perspective alerts the clinician to exhaust empirical medical data provided by the presenting problem and gathered in the patient's history. A recent physical examination is necessary for any disorder that may have somatic roots. Dr. M.'s knowledge of Sally's behavior was grounded in a careful history taking, which indicated that a major mental illness had afflicted the patient's mother. While certainly the illness could have affected the mother-daughter relationship in many ways (e.g., making the mother less emotionally available), Sally's bipolar disorder might also have genetic components.

The disease perspective correspondingly alerts the clinician not to rush prematurely to establish an etiology rooted in a "meaningful explanation" of the problem. For example, it would be facile to attribute Sally's behavior to some fault in the marriage or to personality factors such as inappropriate dependence on male approval. Indeed, almost all depressed individuals attribute their depression to life situations, in an understandable attempt to develop a rationale for the way they feel. It is much easier to say "I am depressed because of the way my life has gone recently" than to say "While things have not been perfect, all in all everything has been going as it usually does. It is just that my depressed mood has a life of its own. My neurotransmitters must not be working properly." The former is an attempt at a meaningful explanation (to be examined in the life story perspective; see Chapter 6), while the latter is a (rarely heard) appreciation of the depression from the disease perspective.

The disease perspective is, as would be expected, the main perspective of schools of medicine and nursing. These graduate programs stress the need to observe carefully and exhaustively the various somatic phenomena in a person's complaint as well as the medical history that he or she provides. Medical graduate programs teach their future clinicians how to conduct a review of organ systems and mental status examinations. Personal and family medical histories yield information about past diseases, surgeries, and medications.

Graduate schools of psychology and social work often do not share this emphasis. In these disciplines, the circumstances of intrapsychic, interpersonal, and social environment are valued highly and therefore often described in minute detail. Attention may be paid to personal and family medical and psychiatric histories. There is less likely to be a recording of the complete regimen of medications with accurate dosage. And conducting a mental status examination — with its attention to factors such the patient's appearance, neurovegetative symptoms, manner of speech, thought processes — is usually an indication that the psychologist or social worker has been trained in a medical or residential facility.

Whereas medical and nursing students may overlook the psychological and relational factors in the patient's disease, social science students, especially with the advent of social constructionism, may overlook the role of the body and the body's diseases in the etiology of the problem. The disease perspective, then, is the familiar territory of the physician, nurse, and medical clinician. It is the terra incognita of the psychologist, social worker, and counselor, unless efforts are made to learn more of this "body" of knowledge. Thus, the role of the disease perspective should be supported and nurtured by the psychologist, social worker, and counselor by developing relationships with medical practitioners, including psychiatrists, who can supplement their psychological skills with medical knowledge of the body and its diseases.

DRUGS, SEX, AND THE DISEASE PERSPECTIVE

Drugs (medically prescribed, alcohol, nicotine, caffeine, illicit drugs) are consumed to cure, to calm, to stimulate, or to avoid physical and psychological pain. The body affected by drugs is a body with altered sexual responsiveness. Therefore, ingested drugs must be recognized as possible causes of sexual dysfunctions and disorders.

Some drugs are alleged to be prosexual in that they are thought to promote sexual activity. Alcohol, cocaine, and hallucinogens, including amphetamines, fall into this grouping. Alcohol is popularly thought to decrease inhibitions about sexual activity. In fact, several researchers over the decades have generally concluded that alcohol has negative physiological effects on arousal and orgasm, to say nothing of the severe health effects that can result from sustained alcohol abuse.(2) But the expectations of both women and men are such that they report increased sexual functioning, even when responding to an alcohol placebo.(3–5) Thus, the frequent clinical situation is that patients generally believe that alcohol helps them to function sexually, while in fact both its short-term and long-term effects on healthy sexual functioning may be the opposite.

Cocaine is a drug of abuse that is often linked with sexual behavior. As is often the case with alcohol intoxication, cocaine impairs judgment and often leads to sexual activity that puts individuals at risk for sexually transmitted diseases. Cocaine's dopaminergic effect increases sexual desire in both men and women but also inhibits orgasm and, given a sufficient dosage, causes erectile dysfunction. Individuals with a cocaine habit will find themselves with increased sexual desire, with little inhibition about the sexual activity, and eventually unable to become aroused.

Hallucinogens such as LSD, Ecstasy, mushrooms, and amphetamines are commonly perceived to be aphrodisiac in their effect on sexual function. This might be expected given the CNS effects caused by these substances. As Crenshaw and Goldberg noted, "The intoxicated states (however mystical) that occur with hallucinogens involve severe alterations in dopamine, serotonin and excitatory amino acid activity. Phencyclidine (PCP, angel dust), for example, incites potent activity at glutamate receptors, apparently inducing psychoses by altering excitatory amino acids. Given the strong impact of these neurotransmitters on sexual function, both extremely positive and negative sexual effects may be

TABLE 2.3
*Some Commonly Prescribed Medications and
Associated Sexual Dysfunctions*

Medication	Sexual Dysfunction Reported
Digoxin	Hypoactive desire and arousal
Diuretics	Hypoactive arousal
Beta-blockers	Hypoactive arousal
Selective serotonin reuptake inhibitors (SSRI)	Hypoactive arousal; delayed or no orgasm
Lithium	Hypoactive desire; hypoactive arousal

expected to occur."(2, p. 192) Relying on intoxication for sexual experience has obvious detrimental long-term consequences.

Other drugs are decidedly negative in their effects on sexual functioning. Excessive alcohol, chronic nicotine use that has caused cardiovascular disease, some antihypertensives, and many antidepressants — all have been implicated in interfering with sexual function. Table 2.3 lists some of the more commonly prescribed drugs and their effects on sexual function. This not an exhaustive list, but it provides examples of the reported sexual dysfunctions associated with the drugs.

Given the various effects that drugs can have on the physiological basis of sexual function, the clinician needs to know what drugs the individual with a sexual problem is taking. A complete review of a patient's use of prescribed, over-the-counter, and possible illegal drugs is essential. Once known, the drugs should be examined for their possible contributory role in the sexual problem. A very helpful resource in determining the sexual effects of medications is MEDLINEplus, a website sponsored by the National Library of Medicine and National Institutes of Health, updated daily; the drug information can be accessed at www.-nlm.nih.gov/medlineplus/druginformation.html. MEDLINEplus, with its wealth of clinical information, can be bookmarked at www.medlineplus.gov.

THE HEALTHY BODY AND SEX

The disease perspective makes sense ultimately when considered against a background of healthy function. Disease is an aberration of healthy cells or physiological functioning. Therefore, the disease perspective on problems of sex must also consider issues relating to the healthy body and sex.

From the viewpoint of physical health alone, sexual activity is exercise and as such is good for the general health of the body. Circulation is increased, muscles stretched, and endorphins released. But as with any exercise, the question may become one of quantity. In other words, is too much sex harmful to the body?

For men, there is a refractory period after ejaculation when a subsequent ejaculation is not possible. The refractory period gradually increases with aging, from minutes in a young man to several hours in an older man. This serves as a natural limit-setting mechanism. For women, dyspareunia — pain with intercourse — is a marker that the vaginal tissue is not prepared for more penetrative activity. The friction of the penis is not assuaged by vaginal lubrication and so pain occurs. Pain may also occur in women and men who manually stimulate their genitals to excess. Pain from abrasions, usually around the glans penis or clitoris, suggests that the skin of the glans is being damaged by too much sexual activity. But apart from the helpful signals of pain — in sexual organs or in other parts of the body (e.g., chest pain) — the effects of sexual activity on a healthy body are comparable to other forms of physical activity: sexual activity is good for the general health of the body.

From the viewpoint of psychological health and social adjustment, the question of too much sexual activity is usually relevant and, to be candid, controversial. Our culture is not one that likes limits — especially sexual limits or limits on what one can do with one's body. From abortion to use of protective headgear for cyclists, any attempt to suggest, let alone legislate, limits on individual choice will be met with heated opposition.

Nevertheless, there is a point at which sexual activity can be detrimental to psychological health and social adjustment. The parallel with exercise is again helpful here. The norm to be used in addressing the question of whether a level of sexual activity is too much is whether the activity interferes with one's psychological maturation or occupational or social functioning. Hours and hours spent in the gymnasium or in a sporting activity daily must detract from the development of other intellectual and interpersonal skills and relationships. Hours and hours thinking about, pursuing, and/or consummating sexual activity must also detract from the development of other intellectual and interpersonal skills and relationships. In this situation, then, too much sex (including thinking about sex) is not healthy for the whole person. I will have more to say about this when discussing the "overvalued idea" in the behavior perspective (see Chapter 4).

Can too little sexual activity hurt the body? There is no evidence that too little or no sexual activity does physical harm to the body. We know that during rapid eye movement (REM) sleep, individuals have a sexual response in terms of vaginal lubrication and erection. It is hypothesized that one of the functions of the lubrication and erection during sleep is oxygenation of the tissues involved.(6) Nighttime sexual arousal may act as a preservative of the tissues necessary for sexual health. In the same self-regulatory manner, nocturnal emissions and ejaculations in men maintain a comfortable level of seminal fluid.

It is common wisdom that most physical activities have a "use it or lose it" factor. Muscles should be stretched; psychological resistance to physical inertia should be routinely surmounted. The same wisdom applies to sexual activity. Especially for postmenopausal women, the normal stretching of vaginal tissues during intercourse serves to preserve suppleness in the vaginal walls. For both men and women, sexual activity usually involves more than the genitals. Torso and limbs move, breathing increases, and the body is exercised. From a physical viewpoint alone, the "use it or lose it" wisdom does have application to sexual activity. Studies of the sexual activity of older persons repeatedly report that the greatest predictor of the level of sexual activity in older age is the amount of sexual activity during the individual's younger years.

MEDICATION FOR THE HEALTHY?

Modern Western culture does not restrict medication to the medically ill. Herbals, dietary supplements, and over-the-counter drugs, as well as highly publicized medications for sexual function such as Viagra (sildenafil) and Cialis (tadalafil), have blurred the categorical boundary between the sick and the well.(7) An extensive review and discussion of the practice of taking such substances is beyond the scope of this book. It is important, however, for the clinician to carefully review the reported effects on sexual function of a substance used by a patient, as available at MEDLINEplus, and to have a clear view of what the substance purports to do in the area of sexual functioning. The distinction between an aphrodisiac and a drug to enhance physiological response is key in this regard.

For example, Viagra and Cialis are not aphrodisiacs. They do not increase one's desire for sex; they augment erectile activity and usually require stimulation — physical and psychic — to be effective. Testosterone, on the other hand, acts on the libido without significantly increasing erectile response. Thus, if a healthy man has erectile dysfunction and a normal testosterone level, there is no reason to give him exogenous testosterone for the erectile dysfunction. In a double-blind, placebo-controlled crossover study, Raul Schiavi and colleagues reported that there was no effect on erectile functioning when testosterone was administered to men with erectile dysfunction.(8) Only a slight increase in ejaculatory frequency was noted, and this was not connected with the participants' self-reports of any increased sense of sexual desire.

The question of medication use by the healthy to enhance sexual function most often arises in connection with the process of healthy aging. The normal aging decrements in function versus the limitations caused by a disease process is a complicated and controversial subject. For an approach to this question, I look at the question of the aging body and sex.

THE AGING BODY AND SEX

From the perspective of a healthy, albeit aging, body, the ability for sexual activity resembles that for any other physical activity. In this view, sexual functioning is similar to jogging, swimming, hiking, and climbing stairs: the more one has done this in the past, the better one is able to do it now and in the future. There may be a general decline in motivation, speed, and endurance, but if essential health is a quality of the aging body, the ability to perform physical activities will remain essentially intact. In the sexual realm, at least for healthy men, a parallel decline in the sensory/neural and autonomic functioning of the genitals is part of the aging process.(9) Erections are slower to attain, briefer in duration; seminal ejaculate is less; and orgasmic pleasure is satisfying but less intense than in earlier years.

Will a healthy older person be able to function sexually? The simple answer is, "The past is prologue," as research studies on sex and aging have taught us. At least for elderly married men, past patterns of sexual activity are strong indicators of sexual vitality in older age.(10) The more complex answer is, "It depends." Whether or not an older person is interested in sex and is sexually active depends on a number of factors other than physical health. Availability of a partner, quality of the relationship, history of sexual expression (or lack thereof), competing interests or commitments (e.g., chosen celibacy) are some of the factors that predict sexual activity in an aging person. These factors are best understood in the life story and behavior perspectives, and I return to examine them in later chapters.

One carefully designed study captures many of the issues involved in sex and healthy aging in men.(11,12) Raul Schiavi, at the time a psychiatrist and sex researcher at Mt. Sinai School of Medicine in New York City, recruited a sample of men (ages 45 to 75) carefully screened to minimize the effects of disease or medications as confounding factors in sexual functioning. Seventy-two heterosexual couples were interviewed, the spouses separately, about their sexual lives together. The men participated in nocturnal penile tumescence (NPT) sleep studies in which erectile tumescence (erection) was monitored with strain gauges attached to the penis. Much to the surprise of the investigators, a high proportion of the men above 65 who failed to have full erections during sleep were, by their own and their partner's independent reports, able to have intercourse regularly and were quite satisfied with their sexual lives.

The strong suggestion in this finding is that compromised physiological status (abnormal NPT) can be overridden by the physical and emotional stimulation of a spouse. The relationship of sex and aging is a complex phenomenon, not given to simple single-cause explanations. While disease processes and "normal" decrements in function are factors to be reckoned with, in real life, many factors enter into the picture. Other perspectives, especially the life story perspective, with its emphasis on value and meaning, need to be employed at this point to give due regard to the complexity of the lives involved.

ILLNESS, INJURY, AND SEX: HEALING RESPONSES

Illness and injury are no friends of good sexual functioning. For some individuals, the loss or decrease of sexual function associated with illness or injury is not really the principal issue. For them, issues of survival, mobility, and financial security dominate their concerns and attention. But for others, the loss of sexual function is an additional major crisis. What had been central in their lives is now gone — or, at best, severely compromised. It seems that those who value sex most in their lives are those who are most distraught by its loss.

Two groups of men come to mind here. In the first group are young men, usually macho men, who have sustained a spinal cord injury from a motorcycle accident or a purposeful gunshot to the sacral spine in an execution-style hit. These young men are devastated by the results of their spinal injuries. For many, the loss of sexual function is the most serious loss they could possibly imagine, let alone sustain. In the second group are older men who have had a radical prostatectomy. If sex has been a central expression in their relationship with wife or partner, then the loss of the sexual function is a major element to be addressed in their recovery from the surgery. A poignant description of this loss and the struggle to rebuild a sexual relationship after prostatectomy is given in Virginia Laken and Keith Laken's autobiographical *Making Love Again*.(13)

Among women who sustain a similar loss are those whose sense of womanhood has been assaulted by illness, injury, or medical or surgical treatment. Surgeries such as mastectomy and vulvectomy, chemotherapies, and colostomies are for some — but certainly not all — women a major challenge to feeling attractive and, perhaps, lovable. Like the men, these women require that the sexual loss be addressed in any comprehensive healing process.

The PLISSIT model of Jack Annon remains, after nearly three decades of use, the most succinct reminder of what role the clinician should play in the healing process of those suffering sexual loss because of illness or injury.(14) *Permission* is given to patients to speak about their sexual concerns by the very act of inquiring with genuine care, "Do you have any concerns about your sexual functioning?" *Limited information* is provided by the clinician, responding directly to patients' questions without overwhelming them with paragraphs of unasked-for information. *Specific suggestions* are often the neglected element of the PLISSIT model. Most recovering patients are greatly helped by specific suggestions on how, *practically,* they can express themselves sexually given the limitations of their conditions. They want to know how they can maximize the sexual function that remains to them. "What do I do with my colostomy so that it won't interfere with him during sex?" "How do I manage a left hemiparesis during sex with my wife?"

Questions such as these do not necessarily mean a referral to the fourth component of the PLISSIT model, *intensive therapy,* as it was traditionally understood. *Intensive therapy* until recently meant a referral to a skilled sex therapist. An alternative and perhaps more effective route for many patients today might be to direct them to peer and professional resources available on the Internet. The leading professional source is the Sexual Health section of the MEDLINEplus website, www.nlm.nih. gov/medlineplus/sexualhealth.html. A commercial site providing expert and peer advice on sexual issues according to illness or injury is www. sexualhealth.com.

SOMATIC TREATMENTS OF SEXUAL DYSFUNCTIONS AND DISORDERS

The most remarkable change in the treatment of sexual disorders in the past two decades has been the emergence of somatic treatments. In earlier years, the only somatic interventions had been surgeries and topical applications. The surgeries included procedures such as insertion of a penile prosthesis and reconstruction of vulvar and vaginal tissue. Topical aids were vaginal lubricants and attempts, usually unsuccessful, to apply an anesthetic to the penis to retard premature ejaculation. In the past twenty years, however, the primary somatic treatment of male sexual dysfunction has been the use of oral medications such as Viagra, intracavernosal injections, and penile vacuum devices. The goal of the treatment is, obviously, to produce an erection capable of penetration. It is an organ-specific goal; there is no claim that the presence of an erection will make the man want to use it sexually — let alone that his partner will want to.

For women, the goal of somatic treatment is likewise directed toward improving the genital environment so that it can contain the penis and respond with pleasurable sensations rather than pain. Vaginal lubricants are sold over the counter and are widely used successfully. For women with hormone deficiencies due to surgery or for postmenopausal women, estradiol vaginal tablets improve lubrication and make the vaginal epithelium thicker. Exogenous androgen is also employed for androgen-deficient women (e.g., those who have had their ovaries removed) to increase sexual desire, but this remains a controversial treatment.(15) A product called EROS-CTD serves as a suction device on the clitoris, improving clitoral engorgement and presumably the potential for vaginal lubrication, subjective arousal, and orgasm. At present, research is being conducted on vasoactive medications for sexual arousal in women, comparable to the Viagra-assisted arousal in men.

A full review of the somatic treatments of sexual dysfunctions and disorders is not the purpose here and is available elsewhere.(16–18). Instead, I offer some comments on somatic treatments from the disease perspective in the context of a typical case.

■ Mark and Esther had been married for thirty-nine years. During the last ten years they had not had intercourse, because of Mark's erectile dysfunction brought on by diabetes. The diabetes was well controlled in recent years, and Mark had felt guilty about not being able to have intercourse with Esther. In preparation for their fortieth wedding anniversary, Mark obtained a prescription for Viagra from his primary care doctor. He tested it privately and, with some manual simulation, obtained a full erection such as he had not experienced in years. He could not wait for their anniversary to surprise Esther.

As might have been predicted by even a casual observer, the anniversary bedroom scene was not a happy one. Having taken the Viagra an hour before retiring, and with some minimal self-stimulation, Mark had a full erection. Esther had reconciled herself years ago to a marriage that was sensual but not sexual. She had not taken hormone replacement after menopause, because she had some medical concerns and, in any case, they weren't having intercourse. Now here they were: forty years of marriage, ten years without intercourse, Mark with a full erection — and Esther with no psychological or physiological preparation for intercourse.

Following some conversation, during which Mark lost the erection, they decided to try intercourse. After some time and stimulation, Mark was able to get an erection. It was difficult to penetrate Esther, and when he finally did it was quite painful for her. He withdrew immediately, with orgasm for neither.

It was about two months before they felt able to seek help, so hurt and embarrassed were they about the failure of communication and the physical pain Mark had caused Esther. The work of the sexual therapy was to assist them to gradually integrate the use of Viagra into their sexual life. It necessitated a switch of focus from his penis to her arousal, both emotional and in terms of vaginal lubrication. After discussing the pros and cons with her internist, Esther began hormone replacement therapy, which made her "generally feel better." Gradually, over a period of four months, the couple progressed in sensate focus therapy, from sensual rapprochement to sexual engagement to successful intercourse about every three weeks.

Integration

The somatic treatments, as briefly described above, offer women and men an opportunity to restore sexual function in situations where disease, surgery, aging, or even psychological factors have made it impossible. These treatments are widely prescribed by primary care physicians and by specialty physicians such as urologists and gynecologists, and many of the somatic treatments are available over the counter. Millions of people will try them; the challenge is whether or not the somatic treatments will be integrated into the sexual lives of those who use them.

The case of Mark and Esther is patently a situation of non-integration in the introduction of Mark's use of Viagra. Mark's attention was too self-focused on the presence of an erection. He forgot that coming together sexually, for two people who care for and are committed to each other, entails more than an erect penis. He was probably totally ignorant of the possible condition of his wife's postmenopausal vagina in the absence of hormone replacement.

Integration of somatic treatments of sexual dysfunction recognizes that the treatments are directed to the genital organs. Their effect is to make the genitals capable of responding sexually. The work of integration is to harmonize improvements in physiological functioning of the genitals with an emotional desire and readiness for the sexual activity. This integration does not require professional assistance for most couples — most can incorporate the somatic treatments into their sexual life through open communication with each other. But other couples, such as Mark and Esther, find themselves unable to use the somatic advances without professional assistance in the work of integration. The art of sexual therapy with such a couple is to provide assistance while being as unobtrusive and noninvasive of their sexual and intimate life as possible. Sexual therapy entails assisting couples to do the work of emotional, sensual, and sexual integration.

Disease

Diabetes and normal aging (menopause) are two real somatic conditions that affected Mark and Esther's ability to function sexually. As such, the diabetes and postmenopausal conditions deserve to be the object of somatic treatment. Perhaps other, psychological interpretations might have been developed to understand their sexual problems. Mark might have been passive aggressive in not treating his erectile dysfunction sooner. Esther, as a consequence of her sense of rejection, might have refused hormone replacement treatment as a way of withholding herself as a potential sexual partner. And there certainly may have been numerous nonsexual marital tensions or differences that could serve as the focus of lengthy marital therapy. But Mark had diabetes and Esther had atrophic vaginal walls.

The disease perspective says that the clinician should first examine all the somatic conditions and diseases that might play a causal role before rushing on to a more psychological understanding of the sexual dysfunction. For the physician, this is professionally instinctive; for the nonphysician with a treatment quiver filled with psychological approaches and interpretations, ruling out diseases and somatic conditions is usually a skill deliberately learned. Nonphysician mental health providers must develop a level of knowledge about the diseases affecting sexual function that is superior to that of the educated layperson. They must also have a good working relationship with primary care physicians, urologists, and gynecologists, both for their own continuing education and for mutual patient referrals.

The Past Is Prologue

In the somatic treatment of sexual dysfunction, it is important to observe the limits posed by premorbid sexual function. "Past is prologue" in the sense that the baseline level of sexual function for the years preceding the onset of the disease is probably going to be the optimum level of functioning possible with the most successful of somatic treatments. A common medical phrase is "return to baseline": the patient returns to the level of function (e.g., cardiac, pulmonary) that he or she had before a disease or critical event.

Mark and Esther will in all probability never have more interest in sex or more frequent sex than they did before the onset of Mark's diabetes. While the "finding again" of each other sexually will undoubtedly enrich their marriage, after their second honeymoon their sexual life will probably settle into the baseline value they placed on sex twelve years ago. This is realistic, not pessimistic. It is a realism that is aided by the disease perspective, with its sensitivity to somatic limits posed by illnesses and injuries even though much of the baseline of sexual life is determined by factors other than somatic.

These nonsomatic factors make the return to baseline not merely a realistic compromise between ideals and reality but also a goal to strive for. After many decades, aging bodies and the ebbing of all novelty demand that the physiological drive for sex be supplemented by motivations of caring, sensuality, and need for intimacy. Helping couples to recall their baseline level of sexual life gives them a joint goal to aim for. Memory and imagination can be employed to picture the type of sexual life the future may hold for them. The clinician's role is — to use the saying usually applied to parents — to give their patients both ground and wings: the ground of accepting the limitations imposed by somatic conditions; the wings of imagining new meanings and ways of coming together sexually.

Mortal Limits

Biomedical ethicist Daniel Callahan wrote that, in our parent's time, persons used to die of natural causes, but today we no longer have that luxury.(19) Callahan was writing about the frenzied exercise of medicine to keep terminally ill patients alive, at great expense to survivors and society. Commonly, family members and medical teams collude in the work of preventing death at all costs. Callahan commented that, in the medical culture shared by both doctors and patients, "natural causes" of death no longer exist; every death is treated as a preventable failure on the part of medicine.

The truth is, of course, that the body dies. Before death, gravity takes its toll on organs and tissues. What was taut and firm now points south. With aging, bodies get smaller, saggier, and weaker. For many, if not most persons, these hints of mortality are an insult. In response, Western culture is replete with strategies to counter this insult: elective plastic surgery, fat farms, and December-June marriages. The culture of youth is as vibrant as its television advertisements. The limits of mortality are denied.

Against this denial of mortal limits, sex is a sign of life. And so it should be. It requires, as has been said repeatedly here, a minimum level of physiological health. In its procreative expression, sex promises future lives if not future life. But sex can also be used as a device to deny limits that, to borrow Callahan's phrase, are "natural causes." The loss or decline of sexual function is a hint of mortality. There is a distinct value judgment to be made about how attentive one should be to hints of mortality. If one takes the position, as I do, that hints of mortality are part and parcel of life that should be listened to, then one should listen to and accept the limits of sexual function without ceaseless somatic interventions. Employing somatic treatments over and over again to deny eventual mortality does little to enrich the sexual life of a couple. Indeed, it may do much to distract from an appreciation of their total life together during the time remaining to them.

The tragedy of September 11, 2001, gave rise to a cultural appreciation of the limits and fragility of life. Persons about to die called their dear ones on cell phones to express their love in their final minutes. Those of us who were survivors, like survivors everywhere, generally expressed in our grief a greater appreciation of "the important things of life" and an intention to "take time to do the really important things." What made this possible was the terrible shout of mortality rising from the crashes of September 11. We heard our mortality and returned to our lives to live them more intentionally.

On a personal level, the many hints of mortality that an individual or couple receives can, and I suggest should, be used for the same purpose of living more intentionally. While somatic treatments for sexual dysfunction may be part of that living intentionally, they may also be part of a collusion to deny mortality at all costs.

SUMMARY

The disease perspective takes the somatic reality of sex seriously. It states that sex is, at its bedrock, a corporal event. To the extent that disease, injury, surgery, medication, and drugs compromise the physiological functioning of the body, to that same extent sexual functioning may be compromised. The clinician working to understand a sexual problem from the disease perspective evaluates the patient's physical and psychological history as well as his or her family medical and psychological history. Although there may be many psychosocial factors that should be noted and treated in due course, the clinician employing the disease perspective wants to be sure that the body is working as well as it can. If somatic treatments will improve sexual functioning, the clinician informs the patient about them and assists in their integration. When the body signals that it has reached its highest level of sexual functioning given its limitations of disease or aging, the clinician understands that signal and turns to another perspective, the life story perspective, to assist the patient in heeding the meaning involved. I talk more about the life story perspective in Chapter 6.

SEX AND THE
DIMENSION PERSPECTIVE

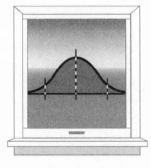

The dimension perspective holds that traits and characteristics are usually normally distributed throughout a population and therefore can be measured dimensionally. An individual may have high, average, or low extraversion, intelligence, and a host of other such traits. When individuals interact within environments that tax the limits of their traits, problems and inadequate responses, including sexual disorders or sexual problems, may result. The dimension perspective calls on the clinician to pay attention to these traits, the particular strengths and vulnerabilities of the individual, in formulating the cause of the disorder and in developing a treatment plan.

AN OVERVIEW OF THE DIMENSION PERSPECTIVE

The dimension perspective is interested in measurement (see Table 3.1). As such, its logic is one of generating numbers and converting them to scores on scales for interpretation by the clinician. The dimension perspective counts and concludes in numbers rather than in categories. For example, the disease perspective is concerned with categories: does this person have hypertension or not? The dimension perspective prefers to ask the question: what are the person's blood pressure readings? The response to the disease question is a categorical yes or no. The answer to the

TABLE 3.1
An Overview of the Dimension Perspective in the Context
of the Other Three Perspectives

Perspective	Logic	What the Patient ____	Treatment
Disease	Categories	Has.	Alleviate or cure
Dimension	**Gradation and quantification**	**Is.**	**Assist in adaptation and response**
Behavior	Goal directed, teleological	Does.	Interrupt, replace behaviors
Life story	Narrative	Encounters and gives meaning to.	Reinterpret or reconstruct narrative

Source: McHugh PR. Managed care and the four perspectives. Paper presented at Academic Behavioral Healthcare Consortium, June 15, 2001.

dimension question is 130/80. Clearly each type of question and response is valid. But each serves a different purpose. Some specific information is lost in the categorization of an individual as, say, "hypertensive" or "normotensive." The exact numerical values are combined into groups according to predetermined cutoff points. There are times when categorical groups facilitate communication—for example, between clinicians who are discussing a patient and between researchers in study design.

In the evaluation and treatment of sexual disorders, the dimension perspective measures three principal domains: personality, intelligence, and the sexual behaviors themselves. This chapter considers all three and suggests how the dimension perspective contributes to the treatment plan.

In overview, the dimension perspective identifies the degrees to which the domains of personality, intelligence, and sexual behavior deviate from the norm. In this statistical distance from the average, the traits indicate either resources to be employed or vulnerabilities to be compensated for in the treatment. The goal of the strategies developed is to assist the individual in adapting to the demands of his or her life situation.

THE DIMENSION PERSPECTIVE APPLIED
TO SEXUAL DISORDERS

Many sexual disorders and problems are rooted in the failure of the individual to respond adequately to the demands of his or her life situation. A timid man is apprehensive about sexual engagement with his partner; he has experienced erectile failure in the past and now worries that this will repeat. An intellectually challenged young woman initiates affection with a new male acquaintance; she is unaware of the sexual signals she is giving to this relative stranger and the possible risk to which she is exposing herself. Both the timid man and the cognitively challenged woman are likely to encounter problems because of the combination of external factors with their unique limitations or vulnerabilities.

The dimension perspective does not attempt to search out the causes of the traits or the behaviors. It is not within the scope of the dimension perspective to ask why the man is timid or what genetic or physiological factors were responsible for the woman's congenital cognitive deficits. Its more modest task is to measure cross-sectionally the personality and intelligence resources available to each individual and to hypothesize how these strengths and vulnerabilities might be expected to respond in the individual's particular life situation.

The dimension perspective also attends to sexual behaviors that have been measured and counted in a population. The prevalence of a behavior (e.g., high-risk sexual behavior) in the population and how frequently it is practiced by different groups of people (e.g., minority adolescents) are of interest to the dimension perspective. Alfred Kinsey initiated this type of data gathering in the 1940s.(1) More recently, and with more advanced scientific sampling resources, epidemiological studies such as the one conducted by Edward Laumann and colleagues at the University of Chicago have provided vast amounts of data that — even a decade later, in the case of Laumann's study — can be mined for the information they provide about sexual behaviors among adults in the United States.(2) Less helpful are the "sex surveys" given banner headlines in the tabloids. These are, in fact, sources of misinformation and faulty generalizations of sexual behaviors.

Reliable and valid inventories have been developed to aid in the dimensional quantification of sexual behaviors and attitudes.(3,4) Table 3.2 lists some that have been carefully developed and used in published research.(5–11) Instruments such as these provide information that either confirms sexual behaviors the patient has reported or adds additional information not gathered in the clinical interview. Both results are helpful. Consistency between the self-report by interview and by inventory lends credibility to the information conveyed by the patient. If there is a divergence between interview and inventory, either the patient was confused about what was asked in the face-to-face interview or in the privately completed inventory, or one of the formats (usually the inventory) provided a safer context in which to report accurately the sexual behaviors in question.

TABLE 3.2

Inventories Measuring Sexual Behaviors

Inventory	Sexual Behavior Measured	Structure of Measure
Female Sexual Function Index, FSFI (5)	Six domains of desire, subjective arousal, lubrication, orgasm, satisfaction, and pain	19 items; self-report
International Index of Erectile Function, IIEF (6)	Multidimensional scale for assessment of erectile function, orgasmic function, sexual desire, and sexual satisfaction	15 items; self-report
Golombok Rust Inventory of Sexual Satisfaction, GRISS (7)	For heterosexual couples: Sexual avoidance, anorgasmia, vaginismus, premature ejaculation, impotence, nonsensuality, dissatisfaction, infrequency, and noncommunication	28 items; self-report
Derogatis Interview for Sexual Functioning, DISF-DISF-SR (8)	Men and women: Sexual fantasy/cognition, arousal, behavior/experience, orgasm, drive/relationship	26 items; self-report or interview
Klein Sexual Orientations Grid (9)	Men and women: Past, present, and ideal rating of seven dimensions of sexual orientation: attraction, behavior, fantasies, emtional closeness, social preference, self-identification, lifestyle	21 items; self-report
Sexual Adjustment Inventory, SAI (10)	Sexually deviate and paraphilic behaviors in male and female adolescents and adults	214 items; self-report; adult and juvenile versions
Child Sexual Behavior Inventory (11)	Sexual behaviors in children who have been (or are suspected to have been) sexually abused	38 items; completed by parent or caregiver

In terms of treatment, the dimension perspective provides information about the strengths and vulnerabilities the individual brings to therapy as well as possible goals of treatment. For example, if the timid man with erectile dysfunction also has high Conscientiousness (as measured by the NEO Personality Inventory–Revised, or NEO-PI-R, discussed below), the therapist can expect him to be diligent about keeping appointments, paying for services, and carrying out behavioral plans, if such are a part of the treatment. The young woman with mental retardation will require treatment interventions that are well suited to her intellectual abilities. Perhaps role-playing will help establish an understanding of how she should respond in various situations with young men. The dimension perspective does not have a specific treatment modality proper to it; it informs whatever the chosen treatment is with knowledge about the patient's resources.

POTENTIAL, PROVOCATION, AND RESPONSE

Given that the dimension perspective is concerned with measurement, the question arises of how these measurements are operationalized. I have already mentioned the interaction between the individual, with his or her array of strengths and vulnerabilities, and the demands of the situation. This is the matrix for operationalizing the dimension perspective. The constructs of individual potential, environmental provocation, and behavioral response comprise the operational triad of the dimension perspective.

An individual with a specific constitutional array of character strengths and vulnerabilities enters a situation in which the environment demands a behavioral response. The response will range from poor and problematic, through adequate, to highly successful, depending on which traits the individual is exercising. Those traits that are well developed will be adaptive and responsive to the situation; those traits that are poorly developed will prove to be sources of problematic responses. A clinical case may help here.

■ George and Millie had been happily married for forty-three years when Millie was diagnosed with cancer. She was ill both with the cancer and with the effects of the chemotherapy for the next two years. During the last two months of her life, Millie was bed-bound, and George, having retired from his position as sales manager with a large industrial firm, was available to care for her twenty-four hours a day. Their love was a great support to them both, although they did not express it sexually during the last year because of the effects of the illness.

One year after Millie's death, George began to date. Six months later he began a relationship with Grace, a woman who was widowed and, with her husband, had been social friends with George and Millie. When they first began to express themselves sexually, George had erectile dysfunction.

George sought therapy immediately, because he did not want anything to interfere with the new relationship with Grace. At the initial evaluation, he completed the NEO-PI-R, a personality inventory.(12) The NEO-PI-R profile indicated, among other traits, that George was high in Extraversion, Agreeableness (very high Altruism subscale), and Conscientiousness. In therapy, he professed no guilt about "being unfaithful" to his deceased wife, and spoke gently about his relationship with Grace. Within two months, George was no longer experiencing erectile problems. The curative factor appeared largely to have been the opportunity to talk about the new relationship in an accepting, nonjudgmental environment. At last contact, George and Grace were planning marriage.

For George, the *individual potential* was the composite of Agreeableness and Extraversion, character traits he had used in caring for his sick and dying wife, in mourning and recovering from her loss, in initiating a social life with women, and in beginning a romantic relationship with one woman. George's high Conscientiousness probably caused his subjective ambivalence about being sexual with a woman other than his deceased wife, and with a woman his wife knew. But his high Conscientiousness also led him to therapy to overcome erectile dysfunction and, finally, to take steps to develop a second committed relationship with a woman. The *environmental provocation* was the illness and death of his wife and, of course, Grace's desire for a committed relationship and marriage. The *behavioral response* was the course of actions described in the vignette.

The dimension perspective suggests that, as a former sales manager and husband of forty-five years, George had the personality traits that facilitated his maintaining a loving relationship (high Altruism) with a woman and being able to initiate a new relationship (high Extraversion). These behaviors — caring for his wife, mourning her death, initiating a new relationship, experiencing erectile dysfunction, resolving the problem, and making a new life commitment — came about because of the alignment of the elements in the specific triad of George's *individual potential, environmental provocation,* and *behavioral response.* The dimension perspective seeks to elaborate this triad in each case, relying on the measurements it provides to describe each element of the triad, but especially the individual potential and the behavioral responses.

THE DIMENSION PERSPECTIVE, SEX, AND PERSONALITY TRAITS

The vignette about George provides an application of measured personality traits for the individual in the midst of a sexual problem. At this point, it might be helpful to describe further some of the associations between personality, sexual behaviors, and clinical groups as reported in the research. I will then return to examine the association between personality and the treatment of individuals with a sexual disorder or problem.

Sexual Behaviors and Group Personality Profiles

The relationship between personality traits and sexual behavior has been examined repeatedly in personality and sexual research, with only modest results in terms of finding correlations between specific sexual disorders and specific personality traits. For the most part, studies have reported on the personality characteristics of sexual offenders.(13,14) Despite multiple attempts to establish a correlation between personality and specific sexual dysfunction, there have been no robust findings such that any specific sexual dysfunction can be associated with any personality profile.

Comorbidity studies of sexual disorders and dysfunctions using Axis II (personality disorder) diagnoses of the DSM-IV-TR examine the question of personality from a pathological perspective. For example, among a sample of pedophilic men, 60 percent met the criteria for a personality disorder, the chief among them being obsessive-compulsive (25%), antisocial (22.5%), narcissistic (20%), and avoidant (20%).(15) Although diagnostic categorical data provide information about personality limitations, they cannot provide the more comprehensive view that a dimensional personality group profile might supply. Knowledge of personality strengths, not merely vulnerabilities rooted in the disorder, are helpful in developing a treatment plan.

An example of a dimensional examination of personality and sexual disorders is found in a study completed in our Sexual Behaviors Consultation Unit (SBCU) at Johns Hopkins. In this study, we found that men with paraphilic behaviors who presented for evaluation and treatment had a distinct group profile as measured by the five-factor personality model of the NEO-PI-R.(12) The clinical sample (N = 51) had high Neuroticism, high Openness to Fantasy, low Agreeableness, and low Conscientiousness. Interpreting these domains suggests that the paraphilic group has a higher than average vulnerability to negative affect. This may have been an artifact of studying a sample from a clinical population, but in any case, the participants in the study described themselves as being chronically distressed. The paraphilic group also had a rich fantasy life. This supports the belief that paraphilia is primarily a cognitive phenomenon that may or may not be amenable to change. The treatment challenge is to assist the patient to avoid acting out the fantasy in criminal or otherwise harmful behaviors. The paraphilic group tended to have a more narcissistic focus and, last, had difficulty in performing consistently and conscientiously in their activities. These latter traits posed distinct treatment challenges that I discuss below.

In contrast to the men with paraphilia, who had a group personality profile with scale scores outside the average range, age-matched men with erectile dysfunction had a group personality profile that was in the average range for each of the five major factors. While certainly many of the individual men had facets and factors that were above or below the average range, for the group no factor was high or low. The pooling of their individual profiles resulted in a regression to the mean. As a result, one cannot predicate any personality traits that may be held in common by men with sexual dysfunction, as was done for the group of paraphilic men.

Two conclusions were drawn from the finding that the paraphilic group had a distinct personality profile and the men with sexual dysfunction did not: (i) some sexual behaviors (e.g., paraphilia) might be correlated with personality traits; and (ii) when no distinct group profile emerges (all scale scores are within the average range), then clinical attention should be directed to the individual personality profile of the patient to see what traits may be contributing to the response of the sexual disorder or behavior. To this task I now turn.

Sexual Behaviors and Individual Personality Profiles

Although sex is usually relational in its expressions, *individual* persons express that sexual behavior. The individual person has enduring qualities and traits that, however they may have developed, shape sexual behaviors and attitudes. Likewise, these same traits may influence the person to react in patterned responses to various influences — both internal and environmental. It is important to assess the relative strengths and vulnerabilities of the traits in the individual with a sexual disorder, so that one can design a treatment program that uses the strengths and minimizes as much as possible the limitations.

While group profiles are helpful in terms of generating hypotheses about the personalities of individuals with a shared sexual behavior, for the most part the contribution of the dimension perspective lies in the attention it pays to the unique array of traits within the individual. Over the past fourteen years, at the SBCU we have used the NEO-PI-R to measure the personalities of individuals with sexual disorders and problems. The NEO-PI-R is not an instrument, such as the Minnesota Multi-

TABLE 3.3

The NEO Personality Inventory: The Five Factors and the Facets That Comprise Each Factor

Neuroticism	Extraversion	Openness	Agreeableness	Conscientiousness
Anxiety	Warmth	Fantasy	Trust	Competence
Angry hostility	Gregariousness	Aesthetics	Straightfor-wardness	Order
Depression	Assertiveness	Feelings	Altruism	Dutifulness
Self-conscious-ness	Activity	Actions	Compliance	Achievement striving
Impulsiveness	Excitement seeking	Ideas	Modesty	Self-discipline
Vulnerability	Positive emotions	Values	Tender-mindedness	Deliberation

phasic Personality Inventory (MMPI), that measures psychopathology. It is, rather, a self-report inventory that yields a profile of the five factors of normal personality structure. The five factors of Neuroticism, Extraversion, Openness, Agreeableness, and Conscientiousness provide a comprehensive assessment of normal personality dimensions. It gives the clinician a picture of the personality of the individual who is seeking help for a sexual problem. Employing a personality inventory such as the NEO-PI-R at the initial evaluation permits the clinician to hypothesize what trait strengths and vulnerabilities may have been involved in the genesis of the sexual problem and what personality resources are available for treatment.

SEXUAL BEHAVIORS AND THE FIVE FACTORS OF PERSONALITY

Each of the five factors of personality has six facets, or subscales, that together comprise the factor (see Table 3.3). Knowing at what level (very low, low, average, high, very high) the individual scores on each of the five factors is helpful, but knowing the thirty facet scores greatly increases the clinical information available to develop or alter a treatment regimen. Our experience of using the NEO-PI-R in a sexual clinic, together with findings from personality/sexual behavior studies, suggests some of the following hypotheses about the relationship between personality and sexual behavior and the treatment of sexual disorders.(16)

Neuroticism and Sexual Disorders

High Neuroticism in general exacerbates the sexual dysfunction or disorder. Depression has long been associated with increased sexual dysfunction. Depression is also associated with an increased likelihood that an individual may act on a paraphilic disorder. An increase in the frequency of fetishistic behaviors is often preceded by increased Depression, Anxiety, or a mixed state of agitated depression. High Selfconsciousness is frequently a component of performance anxiety in which an individual is exquisitely conscious of how he or she is "performing" during the sexual activity.

Low Neuroticism is usually a predictor of dropping out of therapy. Not being distressed, the individual who seeks evaluation for a sexual problem (frequently at the request of a third party) is hard pressed to identify motivating reasons to continue therapy and to pay for it. Often these motivators are rooted in factors of self-interest (e.g., to preserve a relationship in the case of sexual dysfunction, or to preserve an employment position when there has been sexual misconduct in the workplace).

In terms of treatment, too much or too little negative affect is a handicap for therapy. Very high Neuroticism is an indication for the use of psychotropic medications, especially if the patient has a history of affective illness or has abnormal neurovegetative symptoms such as poor or excessive sleep or appetite, low or very high energy. Very low Neuroticism suggests either massive emotional denial or an indifference to the life situations that have brought the individual into treatment. It may be more helpful in this type of case to offer either couple or group therapy. In these modalities, the external conflict that brought the individual into treatment can continue to confront him or her through the interventions of the other group members.

Extraversion and Sexual Disorders

High Extraversion usually promotes sexual functioning.(16) It makes sense that a person who likes to engage in the world will also be disposed to engage in sexual interaction. There are some problematic issues, however, when some of the Extraversion facets become very high. Very high Warmth may be smothering or overprotective and clinging; this may have a negative effect on the partner. The presenting problem will then be one of incompatibility in frequency of sexual intimacy, with the partner appearing to have low desire (for the high Warmth partner) or to be behaving in a passive aggressive manner (which may in fact be so). Very high Excitement seeking is a risk factor in paraphilic disorders, especially those that carry an element of danger to self or others. In individuals with very high Excitement seeking, the risk factor becomes a promotional component in the sexual arousal pattern. In fact, when the risk becomes commonplace, the danger "ante" must be increased to facilitate arousal. Individuals engaged in sadomasochistic behaviors with very high Excitement seeking tend to be especially at risk for personal harm. For some individuals, the danger of contracting HIV is sexually arousing and therefore places the individual at greater risk of contracting the disease.

Low Extraversion is more commonly seen in individuals with sexual dysfunction problems. Low Warmth is associated with sexual aversion disorder, as the individual prefers a more formal and distant relationship pattern — even with his or her partner. The casual, sometimes playful, element of sexual engagement is foreign to a low Warmth interpersonal style. Persons with very low Assertiveness are prone to dependency. When the sexual partner is the object of that dependency, the parity and mutuality that should exist between sexual partners is deficient. This flaw in the basic relationship often promotes a variety of sexual dysfunctions. When very low Positive emotions is coupled with high Neuroticism, there is often a dysthymic disorder with its attendant low sexual desire.

Openness and Sexual Disorders

Like high Extraversion, high Openness tends to promote sexual functioning.(16) The clinical issue for high Openness, therefore, is whether the sexual behavior in question is one that the treatment seeks to promote or seeks to decrease, control, or stop. High Fantasy is common in individuals with paraphilia.(17) As discussed for the SBCU study of fifty-one paraphilic men, this supports the hypothesis that the paraphilic behavior is the acting out of a primary paraphilic fantasy. High Openness to Actions is a positive sign in the treatment of sexual dysfunction. It suggests that the individual is open to trying new sexual scripts that can replace behaviors that for one reason or another have become dysfunctional. This may be as minor as an openness to altering the time of day of sexual engagement.

Low Openness is, conversely, marked by a more confined and rigid sexual pattern or script. It is generally a poor prognostic indicator for the treatment of sexual dysfunction. In such an individual, there is a paucity of sexual fantasy to augment sexual arousal (low Fantasy), a poor appreciation of the subtleties of sexual pleasuring (low Aesthetics), an oppositional set to accepting suggestions from the partner (low Openness to Actions), and a rigid cognitive set about what is right and wrong in the morally charged range of sexual behaviors (low Openness to Values). In terms of reducing the frequency of or stopping a paraphilic behavior, low Fantasy in an individual with paraphilia may be a good prognostic indicator for stopping the behavior. If the individual with low Fantasy avoids the external trigger situations (e.g., places or visual stimuli), this relatively inactive fantasy life is less likely to prompt him or her toward the unwanted behaviors.

Agreeableness and Sexual Disorders

Besides the Extraversion factor, Agreeableness is the other factor describing the individual's interpersonal style. Because sexual expression is such an interpersonal behavior, Agreeableness has much to do with the relational context in which the sexual engagement occurs. If the relationship is hostile, selfish, and nonempathetic, the sexual behavior will occur without those emotional components. While this may suffice for commercial and perhaps recreational sex, it will not be sufficient for caring and committed sexual engagement.

High Agreeableness facilitates sexual activity that is generous, caring, and mutual. Individuals with high Agreeableness tend to trust the other as one who will be caring (high Trust). They are able to speak to the other about their own sexual or pleasure needs (high Straightforwardness). They care for the other's emotional and sexual needs (high Altruism) and are not particularly concerned about always having sex under the conditions (time, place, activity) they would prefer (high Compliance).

Low Agreeableness has just the opposite association with the relational context of sexual activity. Individuals with low Agreeableness tend to see the other as a potential foe (low Trust) on whom they must work their wiles (low Straightforwardness) to wrest from the other the ego-gratifying pleasures they desire. Paraphilic men have low Agreeableness.(17) Sexual offenders have reported interpersonal behaviors that are manipulative and self-gratifying at the expense of their victims.(18)

Treatment of sexual dysfunction and disorders in individuals with low Agreeableness must recognize their narcissistic vulnerabilities. Treatment goals should be framed in terms of their self-interest (e.g., to keep the relationship or employment) and should move to develop empathy for the partner or victims only as rapidly as the abilities of the patient will allow. It is very important to remember that narcissistically impaired individuals are just that — impaired in their abilities to develop empathetic relationships. The clinician may be repulsed by the "selfishness" of such an individual, but a simplistic moralizing is not a stance the competent or ethical clinician can afford to assume. The "demanding" husband and the "predatory" priest with pedophilia may be socially offensive, but they are primarily patients for the mental health clinician. If the therapist has negative reactions (negative countertransference) to the patient with low Agreeableness, that therapist should obtain supervision or refer the patient to a colleague skilled in treating patients with narcissistic personality disorder.

Conscientiousness and Sexual Disorders

Conscientiousness is the factor that measures individuals' ability to set goals and work to achieve them, to adhere to their moral compass (conscience), and, in general, to live a productive and contributory life.

High Conscientiousness generally is a good prognostic sign of cooperation in a treatment or therapy regimen. An individual with high Conscientiousness has the innate ability to set goals and to stay the course until the goals are reached. Problems with sexual behaviors may occur in those individuals with very high Conscientiousness, because of their perfectionist standards imposed on their own sexual functioning. Very high Conscientiousness suggests a rigid set of standards and a dogged perseverance toward goals. These personality traits do not easily mesh with the nondemanding, relaxed interpersonal milieu that partners ideally have as they begin to encounter each other sexually. In sensate focus therapy, the therapist may need to help individuals differentiate between "making" love and the other "makings" that their other life responsibilities demand of them.

Low Conscientiousness, deficits in setting goals and achieving them, is one of the personality marks of men with paraphilic disorders.(17) It may be hypothesized that the psychological energy needed for the tasks of average or high Conscientiousness is being siphoned off in erotic directions. This is not to say that those with paraphilia cannot be high-functioning individuals, holding executive positions. Often in such cases, the paraphilia may serve as an escape from the anxiety inherent in occupational demands or familial duties. For example, men with a transvestitic fetish often look forward to coming home and "getting in drag" as an "island of repose" after a difficult day of workplace decisions and conflicts. Low Conscientiousness, however, suggests that in some way the individual is not living up to his or her potential in all aspects of life's responsibilities.

Low Dutifulness and low Deliberation are of particular concern for those whose paraphilic behaviors have nonconsenting victims. Making moral exceptions for oneself—or not even considering the moral implications of one's behaviors (low Dutifulness) — and making impulsive decisions with little regard for the consequences (low Deliberation)are two hallmarks of the antisocial personality. There is high risk for recidivism in individuals who are sexual offenders and have an antisocial personality disorder.(19)

In individuals with low Conscientiousness, meeting the regimen and responsibilities of a therapeutic contract will pose a challenge. The therapist should expect missed appointments, tardy bill payments, and issues of noncompliance. In a behavioral treatment program such as sensate focus therapy, the frequency of not performing the home exercises will be higher than average when one of the partners has low Conscientiousness. A review of the personality profile of a new patient with low Conscientiousness is often helpful in establishing the mutual awareness that these challenges may arise is therapy. Before they do arise, the specific consequence for each should be made known to the patient. For example, the patient incurs full financial responsibility for an unexcused missed session; or if there is poor compliance with sensate focus therapy, the modality is renamed marital therapy rather than sexual or sensate focus therapy and no home exercises are contracted for.

To summarize the therapeutic approach of the dimension perspective regarding personality traits: if vulnerabilities in personality contribute to unwanted sexual behaviors, then the appropriate therapeutic approach is to address these traits with the goal of compensating for them or redirecting them. For example, if a man uses female prostitutes because his interpersonal skills are ineffective for experiencing intimacy with a woman, he can be helped by the psychoeducational experience of group therapy that focuses on these skills. If, on the other hand, the use of prostitutes is due to high sensation-seeking behaviors, then the desire for excitement and risk should be redirected (sublimated) into more appropriate venues. In either case, it is important to recognize that while a man may attribute his use of prostitutes to "my high sex drive," the far more salient factors may be rooted in his personality traits. The dimension perspective addresses the personality traits as the primary treatment focus, with the working hypothesis that the unwanted sexual behaviors are promoted by these vulnerabilities.

SEXUAL BEHAVIORS AND INTELLIGENCE

If personality traits influence the expression of sexuality, it is reasonable to assume that intelligence, a construct more frequently measured than successfully described, also influences sexual behavior. Intelligence is positively correlated with the Openness factor in personality. As a result, the more intelligent the individual, the more expansive are his or her interests and curiosity in general. In support of this assumption, the National Health and Social Life Survey (NHSLS) reported that higher education level (after high school) was positively correlated with greater frequency of masturbation, oral sex, anal sex, and same-gender sexual partners.(2) At least as measured by education level, the higher the intelligence, the greater the variety of sexual experiences that can be expected in an adult population. Other covarying factors are involved in this positive correlation between sexual behaviors and education level, but the effect of intelligence on envisioning a broad range of sexual behaviors is a reasonable assumption.

Intelligence means not only an openness to variety of sexual experience but also a greater awareness of the consequences of sexual behaviors, thus complementing the variety of openness with a self-regulatory function. This has been observed in populations where sexual behaviors present some risk to self or others. In a study that sampled three hundred seventh to twelfth graders from a population of twelve thousand teens in the National Longitudinal Study of Adolescent Health, investigators at the University of North Carolina found a significant curvilinear relationship between intelligence and whether or not the teen had had intercourse.(20) Adolescents at the upper and lower ends of the intelligence distribution were less likely to have sex. Those with higher I.Q. were more likely to postpone the initiation of the full range of partnered sexual activities. While the higher I.Q. group may have had a greater knowledge of possible consequences, those in a lower I.Q. group may have had less social status for partnered sex. In an earlier study, another University of North Carolina research group also found that adolescent girls with a higher verbal I.Q. had a greater locus of control regarding contraceptive practices.(21)

Intelligence, then, seems both to widen the possibilities of the variety of sexual behaviors over an adult's lifetime and to carry with it the ability to foresee possible negative effects of sexual actions. How this awareness is processed and heeded by an individual rests with a multitude of other personal and situational factors. I recall, for instance, the sobbing distress of a college sophomore who had just learned she was pregnant, "But I can't be pregnant. I get all A's." The tragic assumption was that somehow her intelligence in itself would protect against unwanted consequences of her sexual behaviors.

Low intelligence combined with offensive sexual behaviors poses a distinct risk for recidivism among sexual offenders.(22) The ability to see the consequences of actions in a larger context than the press of immediate gratification or the expression of rage (as in rape) is a function of general intelligence. It is important to assess intelligence quantitatively in all cases with the slightest possibility that the offender may have a below-average I.Q. With this knowledge, the clinician not only can more accurately assess a person's level of responsibility but can develop treatment programs appropriately adapted to the cognitive limitations of the mentally deficient offender.

Apart from the sexual offender population, individuals who are mentally retarded have major challenges in the expression of sensuality and sexuality. The difficulties range from public masturbation in the more severely retarded to the risk of unwanted pregnancy in those who are unaware of the possible consequences of sexual intercourse. It is the responsibility of the parents, guardians, and institutional care-takers of mentally retarded individuals to take special steps to educate them about sexual matters. Both intensive group and individual efforts have been helpful in assisting the mentally retarded individual to understand the basic parameters that govern sexual behavior. For example, "We do not rub our genitals (penis, vulva) in public. We do not touch another in private places unless that person gives us permission to touch." The first and perhaps the most difficult step in providing appropriate sex education and corresponding social skills to the mentally retarded is to overcome any reluctance that parents, guardians, and institutions may have in addressing the sexual issues of their children and residents.

Individuals with autism and pervasive developmental disorders such as Asperger syndrome are also at risk for sexual problems.(23–25) There have been anecdotal reports of paraphilic behaviors in individuals having these developmental disorders that affect social intelligence. It is reasonable to hypothesize that, because of their impaired ability to develop intimate social relationships, individuals with autism or Asperger syndrome are more likely to develop patterns of sexual expression that are not incorporated within loving and caring relationships. At the present time, however, systematic research has revealed little about the sexual problems of individuals with these disorders. Despite this paucity of knowledge, the dimension perspective alerts the clinician to be aware of possible sexual disorders and problems when treating such patients.

Dementia, particularly the Alzheimer type, can be associated with problems of sexuality. While episodes of sexual disinhibition are what cause neighbors and staff of residential facilities to become concerned, if not alarmed, the far more common problem is hypoactive sexual disorder. Connected with this low desire is the distress of the partner of a person with dementia. What partners often report and are saddened by is the impersonal and "stony" quality of the lovemaking of their partners. What had throughout their life together been an occasion of intimacy may now be reduced to an episode of physiological release. In dementia, the decreased ability of memory and interpersonal sensitivity — so closely connected with intimacy — impairs the expression of tender sexuality. On the other hand, sexual expression between partners, one of whom may be severely demented, may be the final link as two bodies experience primary touching and holding that is precortical in its perceptions. A wonderful description of this connectedness is elaborated in the novel *The Notebook,* by Nicholas Sparks.

In the process of developing a treatment plan for an individual with cognitive limitations and with a sexual disorder or dysfunction, clinicians often do not have the luxury of the results of a Wechsler Adult Intelligence Scale (WAIS) or other standardized intelligence measures. Clinicians do, however, have the ability to make an effort to judge the patient's intelligence. This can be done by noting education level, occupation, level of vocabulary, and, if there is a question of borderline cognitive abilities, the manner in which the individual interprets proverbs. The dimension perspective assists the clinician to judge intelligence and to support that judgment with clinical data. The treatment plan is then adapted to the patient's cognitive level.

SPECIAL GROUPS AND THE DIMENSION LOGIC

Age and the Dimension Perspective

When the chronological age of the patient is considered in the formulation of a case, the dimension perspective is being employed. As noted earlier, the dimension perspective uses the logic of gradation as opposed to categories. The units of measurement in the construct *age* are, of course, the integers of months and years. Age may play an important role in the formulation for a patient with a sexual problem or disorder. For example, during the course of taking sexual histories with two separate individuals, the clinician learns the following:

1. Jason, a 15-year-old adolescent, reported that he masturbates about three times a week.
2. Max, a 55-year-old married man, reported that he masturbates about five times a day and has intercourse with his wife about once a week.

Without being conscious of it, most clinicians would employ the dimension perspective to integrate these facts into their formulation of the cases. The constructs being measured are age and masturbatory behavior. Age has been measured as 15 and 55. For each patient, his age is placed against the distribution of lifetime expectancy of 78 years. The interacting variable with age is masturbatory behavior, measured at three times weekly for Jason and five times daily for Max. These frequencies are placed in the normal distribution of frequency of masturbation in males according to age. No ready data source is available for the normal distribution of masturbation frequency, but studies such as the NHSLS(2) suggest that Jason's masturbation behavior falls within the expected frequency range for young men and Max's is at the extreme high end of the distribution curve for middle-aged men. With this information, the dimension perspective contributes to the formulation of each case with a conclusion about the masturbation frequencies of each patient.

1. Jason has a masturbation frequency within normal expected limits.
2. Max has an exceptionally high masturbation frequency.

This procedure may seem obsessive for reaching what is a fairly straightforward clinical impression. What is important to note, however, is the methodology involved. First we determined the behavior or construct to be measured: age and masturbation. Then each was measured. We then compared the measurements with distribution data from available research. Finally, we interpreted the outcome of the two variables of interest, age and masturbation, on the distribution curve and came up with a clinical judgment. This is the logic of measurement and gradation employed in the dimension perspective.

The dimension logic does not, in itself, make value judgments about the behaviors or constructs it measures. It can, and of course does, contribute to value judgments made by patients, clinicians, and society at large. The logic of the dimension perspective relies on good research. In sexual behaviors, it relies on a body of research that is neither as comprehensive nor as robust as one would like. There is a need for more research about the epidemiology of human sexual behaviors that is peer reviewed and available to scholars and public alike.(26)

Sexual Orientation and the Dimension Perspective

In addition to personality traits, intelligence, age, and sexual behaviors, the dimension perspective can contribute to an understanding of an individual's sexual orientation. This is obviously not a new thought. In 1948, Alfred Kinsey and colleagues wrote, "The world is not to be divided into sheep and goats. Not all things are black nor all things white. It is a fundamental of taxonomy that nature rarely deals with discrete categories. Only the human mind invents categories and tries to force facts into separated pigeon-holes. The living world is a continuum in each and every one of its aspects. The sooner we learn this concerning human sexual behavior the sooner we shall reach a sound understanding of the realities of sex."(1, p. 639)

Most people, however, look at sexual orientation from a categorical rather than a dimension perspective. They place individuals neatly and distinctively into three categories: heterosexual, homosexual, or bisexual. Such categories are employed in conversation as nouns, not adjectives: "He is a homosexual" or "She was a bisexual but now is a lesbian." Even much research on sexual orientation usually employs categories, homosexuals versus heterosexuals, in its design. This research design makes the group analysis of the data much more efficient, but it may do so at the cost of valid results (e.g., overlap of group membership). While categories are handy and easy to employ in everyday speech and research, they may not be our best way to convey the complexity of what we are speaking about or studying. The dimension perspective, with its logic of gradation and measurement, holds a complementary, but corrective, viewpoint in the discussion of sexual orientation.(27)

Just as Kinsey and co-workers urged in 1948, with their seven gradations of sexual orientation, the observations of the NHSLS suggest that matters may not be so simple as a threefold categorical approach to sexual orientation. In the NHSLS, Edward Laumann and colleagues measured three dimensions of homosexuality: same-gender sexual behavior, same-gender sexual desire and sexual attraction, and self-identity as a homosexual person. Their results indicated that in any one individual these three dimensions may or may not be consonant. The NHSLS reported that 2.8 percent of men and 1.4 percent of women in the study identified themselves as homosexual or bisexual, while 7.7 percent of men and 7.5 percent of women reported same-gender attraction or interest. In terms of same-gender sexual behavior, 2.7 percent of men reported behaviors in the past year and 4.9 percent since 18 years of age. Among women, 1.3 percent had same-gender behavior in the past year and 4.1 percent since 18 years of age.(2) Thus, while for most individuals there is a consistency between self-identity as homosexual or bisexual and attractions to the same or both genders, for others there may be attractions to and sexual activities with same-gender partners and yet no self-identification as homosexual, lesbian, or bisexual. A dimension perspective captures this more nuanced description of the individual's sexual orientation, as this dimension separately measures sexual self-identification, sexual attractions, and sexual behaviors.

■ For 44-year-old Robert, life had reached a nadir as he sat slumped in the chair at the therapist's office. He reported that his wife had discovered him making a phone call to Marty, a 22-year-old sex-for-hire man whose services he had purchased infrequently over the past three years. The marriage was in crisis. His wife feared HIV infection and was threatening to make the behavior public in a divorce. He had tried to stop the sexual contacts with Marty previously and failed. Robert loved his wife and valued his role as the father of their three children. He was clearly devastated.

He described his sexual contacts with Marty. They met in Marty's apartment. There was little talking before or after Marty performed fellatio on him. Money would be exchanged for the sex, and Robert would be back in his car and driving home about fifteen minutes later. He did not know Marty's last name or anything about his personal life. He was not sexually attracted to Marty, nor did he care about him. Robert had found Marty by responding to a personal advertisement in a free city paper.

Before Marty, and throughout the marriage of sixteen years, Robert had had a series of anonymous sexual contacts with men, which began in erotic bookstores. The frequency was about six times a year. When asked to describe the attraction to fellatio performed by men, Robert was uncertain. He liked the sexual pleasure, of course, but in addition, he thought the young men admired his genitals and this gave him a sense of pride. He was repelled by the thought of living a publicly gay lifestyle or the idea of being partnered with a man. The male friends with whom he played golf every Saturday would not understand the behavior and would probably reject him from their circle.

It might be helpful to look at Robert from the dimension perspective. As an instrument to do this, the clinician might employ the Klein Sexual Orientation Grid, an inventory that measures several different dimensions of sexual orientation, in the past, at present, and as the individual would ideally like to be.(9) Fritz Klein and colleagues suggested seven dimensions of sexual orientation: attraction, behavior, fantasies, emotional closeness, social preference, self-identification, and lifestyle. In Robert's case, there is a lack of concordance among the seven. His behavior, attraction, and fantasies are with both men and women. His emotional closeness, social preference, self-identification, and lifestyle are that of a heterosexual married man.

Although the Klein inventory itself may be somewhat cumbersome to use clinically — a common limitation of the dimension perspective — it does identify and measure components within sexual orientation.(28) It reminds the clinician that the categories of sexual orientation are only the starting point for understanding an individual's erotic and social preferences. The clinical question for Robert and his wife may be, "Am I (is he) a homosexual?" Use of a dimension perspective will result not in giving Robert and his wife a simple yes or no but rather in exploring with them the varied and conflicting elements of Robert's erotic life and what he wants to do to resolve or regulate the conflicts. In Robert's case, and in those similar to his, the terms *homosexual, bisexual,* and *heterosexual* are now employed as adjectives qualifying multiple dimensions of sexual orientation. They are not used as nouns to categorize, and frequently to stereotype, the individual.

What, then, are the clinical implications of regarding sexual orientation as dimensional? It means that for some, especially those who have both homosexual and heterosexual attractions, there may be a choice of how and with whom they express their sexuality. In this situation, we are really speaking of sexual preference rather than sexual orientation. If the behaviors are truly ones of preference, then the therapist can work to make those preferences as informed and voluntary as possible. The therapist can assist the patient to foresee and thus to be informed about the likely consequences of sexual choices and the impact of these choices on the lives of others — especially the patient's near and dear ones. The therapist can allow the choice to be as voluntary as possible by addressing the unconscious conflicts (analytic therapy), basic assumptions (cognitive therapy), or management of environmental consequences (behavioral therapy). In many cases, this will allow the patient to live in the sexual orientation that he or she prefers, even though traces of inconsistency may linger for life.

For other individuals, the consistency of the dimensions argues for the use of the word *orientation*. Whether their erotic object pattern was fixed by genes, fetal environment, familial environment, the events of developmental life, or a combination of factors, these individuals have not chosen it as much as discovered it. The therapy process will assist the patient in that discovery with supportive neutrality, typically helping the individual integrate homosexual attractions, behaviors, and identity both intrapsychically and interpersonally.

SUMMARY

Many sexual disorders and problems are rooted in the failure of individuals to respond adequately to the demands of the life situation in which they find themselves. The dimension perspective urges the clinician to assess (measure) a patient's various strengths and vulnerabilities that are contributing to the failure of response. Personality traits and intelligence are the principal dimensions to be assessed for resources and weaknesses. In sexual matters, it is helpful to measure the frequency, duration, and intensity of the sexual behaviors against norms, to the extent that the limited research allows. The dimension perspective is not used to understand etiology — the disease and life story perspectives are more appropriate for this task — but rather is employed to give a clear and, if possible, quantified picture of how the individual cognitively, socially, and emotionally relates to his or her world.

■ 4

SEX AND THE BEHAVIOR PERSPECTIVE: PROBLEMATIC BEHAVIORS

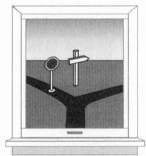

Sexual behaviors can be among the most intimate joys experienced by men and women. The delights of erotic love and sexual behaviors have been praised in the Song of Songs in the Hebrew Scriptures; extolled and taught in the Kama Sutra; and sung about in the Renaissance music of lute and harp and, in our day, in the noise of boom boxes.

But sexual behaviors — or their absence from a relationship — can also be very problematic. Betrayed relationships, sexual assaults, sexually transmitted diseases, and domestic violence can often be the result of sexual behaviors that produce more pain than pleasure, more injury than intimacy. The behavior perspective assists the clinician in looking seriously at problematic sexual behaviors and in addressing what is lacking or misdirected in their expression.

AN OVERVIEW OF THE BEHAVIOR PERSPECTIVE

The behavior perspective is concerned with the actions of an individual that are goal directed and purposeful (see Table 4.1). This perspective looks at what a person does and, if the behavior is problematic, develops treatment strategies that will interrupt or replace it. Unlike the dimension perspective, the behavior perspective requires an exploration into the causes, usually called antecedents, of the behavior. It is also occupied

TABLE 4.1
*An Overview of the Behavior Perspective in the Context
of the Other Three Perspectives*

Perspective	Logic	What the Patient _____	Treatment
Disease	Categories	Has.	Alleviate or cure
Dimension	Gradation and quantification	Is.	Assist in adaptation and response
Behavior	**Goal directed, teleological**	**Does.**	**Interrupt, replace behaviors**
Life story	Narrative	Encounters and gives meaning to.	Reinterpret or reconstruct narrative

Source: McHugh PR. Managed care and the four perspectives. Paper presented at Academic Behavioral Healthcare Consortium, June 15, 2001.

with the consequences of the behavior — both those that reinforce the behavior and those that tend to inhibit its repetition.

The behavior perspective invites the clinician and patient to focus on the conditions that maintain expression of the behavior rather than on what may have started the behavior initially. The perspective draws from all dimensions of the biopsychosocial world in its work to identify the antecedents and consequences of a behavior. Therefore, the other three perspectives (disease, dimension, and life story) contribute to understanding the antecedents of the behavior.

Not surprisingly, the treatment approaches (discussed in Chapter 5) are those that would be identified as behavioral or cognitive-behavioral. The behavior perspective is particularly helpful when problematic behaviors have become "habits," "compulsions," or "addictions." Behaviors that have a motivational component of physiological drive (e.g., eating, drinking, sexual behavior) are those best understood and treated using the behavior perspective as the primary approach.

WHAT IS SEXUAL BEHAVIOR?

When we hear the word *sex,* it is sexual behavior that usually first comes to mind. Good sex, bad sex, no sex — these terms usually refer to some sexual behavior that is performed or not performed, as the case may be. The first question to be addressed in the behavior perspective on sexual disorders is, what do we mean by *behavior*?

First of all, it is important to narrow our definition of *behaviors.* As here defined, behaviors are not equivalent to actions. Actions are bodily movements such as hiccups, falling out of bed, having a heart attack. Actions are not voluntary activities. Behaviors, on the other had, are goal-directed activities. They are activities carried out by the individual that are directed toward some purpose, goal, or object. In that sense they are teleological. Centuries ago, the Roman canonists made a distinction between actions and behaviors. They referred to an action as *actus hominis,* an act of a human (man); to behaviors as *actus humanus,* human activity. The adult person was morally responsible for each *actus humanus,* but not so for each *actus hominis.* In a sexual context, a nocturnal emission during an erotic dream is a human action but not a human behavior. A man sitting perfectly still while imagining a sexual encounter is engaging in a human behavior, even though the activity is almost exclusively cortical.

This is an important distinction, because mental health specialists have an interest in the responsibility of the individual for his or her sexual behavior. Responsibility, literally the ability to respond, is necessary for society's and the individual's understanding of the behavior in question. It is also a requirement for establishing a therapeutic plan. While unwanted sexual behavior might be described by the subject or others as compulsive, addictive, sinful, illegal, or habitual, at some level there is an element of choice. The individual chooses to perform the behavior. At this point, the humanity of the behavior exists.

At some level of awareness, then, the individual says, "I want this and I will do this sexual behavior." We know, however, that no choice is made in a vacuum of pure rationality. There are forces (physiological drives, memories, unfulfilled longings, and so forth) that shape the content and form of any behavior, including sexual behavior. And motivational factors influence the freedom of rational choice in every behavior, certainly in sexual behaviors.

There is a difference between saying that a behavior is involuntary and saying that antecedent factors influence the expression of the behavior. When, in a court procedure, someone is deemed to be not criminally responsible, that person is judged to be, at the time of the criminal action, either unaware of the difference between right and wrong or unable to conform his or her behaviors to the dictates of the law. This is clearly a situation in which the activities of the person have violated the laws of society, but not one in which that person had sufficient capability to choose to perform a purposeful, goal-directed behavior. The mental state of the individual was such that he or she could not choose to do a behavior.

When we refer to sexual behavior in the behavior perspective, however, we refer to behavior that at some point in its elaboration entails an element of choice. The individual says on some level of consciousness, "I will do this." We assert, then, an element of voluntary choice in every sexual behavior, although not in every sexual activity (e.g., sexual activity as a product of a manic state in a bipolar disorder). The volition of the behavior might be compromised by conditions that are antecedent to the behavior and that play a major role in the expression of the behavior, but a choice is made at some point by the individual. This is a basic assumption of the behavior perspective.

ANTECEDENTS, BEHAVIORS, CONSEQUENCES

Having made the important distinction between sexual behavior and sexual activity, we can use an easy mnemonic device to provide a fuller description of behavior. It is the "ABC" of behavior: antecedents, behaviors, and consequences. *Antecedents* are all those factors that precede the behavior: physiological drives and acquired influences that are both internal (e.g., drugs, beliefs, attitudes) and external (e.g., environmental). The *behaviors* are the presexual and sexual behaviors that constitute the behavior in question. The *consequences* are the results of the sexual behavior, that is, all those conditions that are attributable to the performance of the sexual behavior. In many circumstances, the consequences become the antecedents of the subsequent behavior.

■ John was referred for evaluation as a condition of employment, after his firm's information systems department discovered he had been using the Internet to access explicit sex sites during the workday. John had been married for twenty-four years, and throughout his marriage he had struggled against attractions to young, muscular women who would assume a dominatrix role. Before his marriage, he told his fiancée about this masochistic component in his erotic life. She would have no part in it, and the matter was never discussed between them again. The marriage had been stable and they now had two grown children.

About two years before being evaluated, John had several major life stressors. His father died and his mother had to be put in a nursing home against her will. His daughter had been treated for cancer and was presently in remission. Work pressures were increasing, as he was being required to increase his production with no real salary compensation.

In this context, John started to access bondage and dominance websites in the privacy of his work cubicle. The behavior grew in frequency, duration, and masturbatory pleasure. At the behavior's peak, John would spend about two hours doing it daily, concluding with masturbatory orgasm at the websites. He felt ashamed of the behavior and that he was becoming more and more "under its control." The behavior pattern terminated only when his employer's information systems personnel discovered the repeated accessing of the websites on work time. John was required to be psychologically evaluated for the behavior as a condition of continuing employment.

The internal antecedents of John's sexual behavior of accessing the Internet were his sexual attraction to young dominatrix women, which he had experienced for his entire adult life but until recently had resisted expressing. The external antecedents were the familial and workplace tensions. At some point—perhaps a moment of exquisite vulnerability because of fatigue or other circumstance—John chose to surf the Internet, stopping at an explicitly sexual bondage and dominance website. By this time, the antecedents had become the behavior. He looked at the content of the website and was sexually aroused. At some point he returned to the website and masturbated to the stimuli he found there. The immediate consequences were sexual pleasure and release of tension; the more remote consequences were the development of a secret sex life and a pattern of sexual expression outside his relations with his wife.

The factors that initially cause a pattern of sexual behavior need not be the factors that maintain it. The first instance of John's surfing the Internet at work had a unique set of dimensions, but all his subsequent returns to the behavior became reinforced by the subjectively positive consequences (sexual pleasure and release of tension), while the less powerful, negative consequences (secret sexual life apart from his wife) served to inhibit the behavior. One "negative" consequence, his shame about the behavior, may in fact have increased John's anxiety and tension, thus establishing antecedents that promoted further expression of the behavior. Unfortunately, while John regretted a secret life apart from his wife, his regret did not outweigh the positive consequences of sexual gratification. As a result, he tended to deny, minimize, and rationalize the negative consequences, thus reducing their possible effect of stopping the sexual behavior.

A process of conditioned learning developed in which John "learned" through the conditions (consequences) of his sexual behaviors that he experienced pleasure and only a minimal amount of internal conflict with his view of himself as a faithful spouse and diligent employee. The conditioned learning process was challenged only when his employer called his behavior into question. At such a point, an individual in John's situation suddenly sees the great gaps in his perception of what he was doing. He had been unaware (psychoanalytically "in denial") of the possible effects of his behavior on himself and his family. With the discovery, his compartmentalization of the behavior was eroded and now he faced the conflicts that had been present though unacknowledged throughout.

ANTECEDENT CAUSES OF SEXUAL BEHAVIORS

The antecedent causes of sexual behaviors are multiple: genetic and physical, sociocultural, developmental, and "reasons of the head and heart" — personal meaning assigned to the behavior. Each plays a role in the elaboration of the sexual behavior and in the development of a pattern of behaviors. In discussing the disease perspective, for example, I suggested ways in which the body (including genetic influences) contributes to the expression of sexual behavior. The life story perspective emphasizes the personal and social meanings attached to sexual behavior. Thus, when we speak from the behavior perspective, we are not jettisoning the other perspectives. Quite the contrary: we are taking from them the insights they provide so as to understand the causes, maintenance, and treatment of the disordered behavior.

Physiological Substrate for Sexual Vulnerability

The question may be asked, what about the pressure of physiological drive on behavior? In other words, how important an antecedent in sexual behavior is the force of an individual's libido? To put the question in a slightly different format that opens up the range of sexual behaviors, is there in the individual a physiological vulnerability that causes, or at least predisposes the person to, paraphilic or compulsive sexual behaviors? Is there just too much testosterone for the proper control of the sexual drive?

The peripheral signals of touch, smell, taste, penile and vaginal engorgement, ejaculation, and vaginal contraction that constitute preorgasmic and orgasmic sexual experience ultimately reach the limbic hypothalamic system of the brain. We do not know how these signals are experienced and interpreted as erotic pleasure, but it is theorized that the mesolimbic pathway provides the conduction for reinforcing pleasures of sexual behavior. The neurons of the mesolimbic pathway release the neurotransmitter dopamine. This system can reinforce behaviors and cause them to be repeated with greater frequency. The pathway may also release endogenous opiates, heightening the intensity of pleasurable sensation. In this sense, further research on sexual behaviors may find that, for some individuals, CNS functions makes them vulnerable to problematic sexual behavior. While the present use of the word *addiction* is usually restricted to the ingestion or injection of an external substance, future research may provide the grounds to speak of an internal addictive response to sexual stimulation.(1) If so, such individual have a physiological substrate in their CNS that is vulnerable to problematic sexual behaviors.

Does this theory move us from the behavior perspective to the disease perspective? Not necessarily. Integrating the knowledge that the disease perspective supplies about the somatic antecedents of sexual behavior into the behavior perspective allows the focus to remain on behavior, but with the added information that in certain individuals some physiological factors motivate the sexual behavior.

An example lies in the role of hormones in sexual behavior. Whether the hormonal milieu is considered positive or negative, facilitative or inhibitory, largely depends on the interaction of hormones with other psychosocial variables. At this point in our knowledge, we know that androgens in both men and women are important factors in sexual interest, desire, and drive. In adolescence, testosterone levels are predictive of the initiation of coitus in both men and women, although social factors, especially church attendance, can play a moderating role in the effect of testosterone in female adolescents.(2,3) In hypogonadism in men and women, bioavailable androgens decrease and so does sexual desire.(4,5) It might be most accurate, then, to think of the age-specific normal androgen levels in men and women as a necessary but not fully sufficient (especially for women) condition of sexual desire.(6) Below the range of normal levels, sexual desire is usually deficient; levels above the normal range have not been shown to result in hypersexual behaviors as judged from studies of sexual offenders, although there is some indication that higher levels of testosterone are associated with more violent sexual offenses.(7,8)

The term *hypersexual disorder* is now being used by some professionals who are quite intentional in their use of psychiatric nomenclature.(9) Does this term, in fact, capture a clinical syndrome that deserves a diagnosis? Should the DSM diagnosis Hypoactive Sexual Disorder be complemented by Hypersexual Disorder? This might be a helpful addition if, as would be consistent with the philosophy of the DSM, the construct is limited to a description of a pattern of behaviors and does not include an implied etiology. As such, Hypersexual Disorder would address a pattern of sexual behaviors that is considered supernormal in frequency, duration, or intensity and has interfered with the individual's occupational or social functioning. Excluded from this diagnosis should be individuals whose behaviors are caused by a somatic abnormality, such as mania connected with bipolar disorder.

Life Story Antecedents

In addition to the physiological drives that are often connected with problematic behaviors, there is another realm of individual experience that motivates behaviors. It is the cognitive context within which the individual places and organizes his or her experiences. Developed in cognitive therapy theory, the cognitive context is often referred to as the "assumptive world" of the individual. The assumptive world develops from the individual's perceptions of life experiences. It forms the organizing structure that makes sense of life and, hopefully, gives it meaning. The assumptive world is composed of cultural or environmental influences, developmental influences, and, in some extreme instances, overvalued ideas.

In the area of *cultural influences*, it is a truism to say that Western culture flaunts sexual content. In addition to advertising and the commercial media, one of the most remarkable cultural factors of the past decade has been the use of the Internet for sexual purposes. Bulletin boards, chat rooms, and for-profit pornography websites are in abundance. According to SexTracker.com, in February 2002 there were 67,530,775 unique visitors worldwide to the sexually explicit websites it monitors. This remarkable statistic alerts us to something absolutely new that has happened in the cultural management of sex.

With the use of the Internet, individuals interact with other people and share sexual fantasies in relative anonymity. Formerly, many thought that their private sexual interest and object of arousal (e.g., watching a woman smoke or eat) was some idiosyncratic desire that they alone had. Now they log on to the Internet and find that hundreds, in some cases thousands, of others share their unusual erotic attraction. The culture of the Internet and its environmental influence both legitimate and promote sexual behavior. When a sexual behavior is unwanted and problematic, these cultural and environmental factors must be countered and minimized to stop the behavior.

It is not my purpose here to delineate the multiple influences of culture on sexual attitudes and thus on behaviors. Gender roles, pair bonding, marriage, monogamy versus polygamy, monoandry versus polyandry, sexual pleasure, intimacy, procreation — all are shaped by the cultural institutions and groups in which an individual lives. These cultural influences are forces that mold the expression or suppression of sexual behaviors. As such, they are part of the life story antecedents of behavior.

Developmental influences on sexual behaviors range from exposure to androgens in utero (biological factors) to lessons taught by parents about sex (psychosocial factors). For example, one of the most remarkable syndromes involving genetics and hormones is androgen insensitivity syndrome. In complete androgen insensitivity syndrome (CAIS), the XY fetus has testes that produce androgens, but other fetal tissues are nonresponsive to them. The fetus, and later the child, converts the androgens into estrogens and develops as a female. By adolescence, she has typical breast and hip development as well as external female genitalia. There are no internal female organs, so menarche does not occur. If the condition has not been identified earlier, this lack of menstruation brings the girl to medical attention. Although CAIS is a syndrome that carries with it psychological challenges, gender identity and confusion about sexual orientation are not usually the problems. The girl — young woman — is convinced she is a female and her orientation is usually heterosexual. All this in an individual with a 46-XY karyotype! The developmental influences of genes and the resultant syndrome are so powerful that the "normal" course of gender identity and sexual orientation expected in 95 percent of XY individuals does not occur. The sexual behaviors later in this individual's life are profoundly influenced decades earlier by a genetic makeup that resulted in CAIS.

More commonly noticed as developmental factors, however, are the values and lessons about sexuality that are experienced as a child. These are developmental influences as we most frequently refer to them.

■ Harriet recalled that when she was 6 years old, her mother slapped her hands severely when she found her masturbating as she went to sleep. In response, Harriet had to promise to sleep with her hands outside the covers and was disciplined in the middle of the night should she be found with her hands under the covers. Now married, she came to the clinic to report persistent and recurrent genital pain whenever she attempted to have intercourse with her husband.

A family in which sexual pleasure is harshly punished (as when a parent "catches" a young child rubbing his or her genitals) is likely to develop children who are alienated from erotic or sexual pleasure. It is not that they do not experience arousal, but they compartmentalize both sexual arousal and orgasm into the nether world of "dirty" pleasures "down there." As a common result, it is difficult to integrate sensual and sexual pleasure into expressions of intimacy with a loved one.

At the other end of the spectrum of sexual attitudes are families in mainstream Western culture that allow and/or encourage a great amount of nudity and excessive sexual expression (verbal and behavioral). These families may be at risk for developing young adults who use sexual behavior for many emotional needs (e.g., anger, boredom, tenderness) without much discernment about the behavior's long-range effects.

■ Andrew was a very successful stockbroker who had had a series of extramarital affairs with his female staff members. The most recent employee to become a target of his attention probably had a borderline personality structure that decompensated (à la *Fatal Attraction*) when Andrew could not meet all her demands for attention. Her phone call to his wife, informing her of their relationship, precipitated the consultation.

In talking about his family of origin, Andrew nondefensively described how he and his siblings engaged in sexual play and during adolescence had girlfriends and boyfriends in the home for sex. Both parents seemed to tolerate this and, in their alcoholism, were preoccupied with other matters. Andrew also described his mother complaining to him about her poor sexual life with his father—clearly an emotional boundary violation of the mother-son relationship. The home had an atmosphere of high "free-floating" sexuality, quite a contrast to its cultural peers.

As Andrew recounted these matters, he made no emotional connection between his present pattern of sexual behavior with employees and his developmental influences. As therapy progressed, he grew in awareness of these factors, but they remained of "intellectual" interest only. Other, more behavioral interventions were necessary to stop the behaviors.

In many ways, individuals such as Andrew use sexual gratification as others use the consumption of food: for psychological and physical self-soothing. For these individuals, the consuming of sex or food soothes anxiety and distress—even when the libido or the gnawing alarm of an empty stomach has not sent promptings to consciousness. The reflexive response to anxiety is to eat or to have sex. While usually attributed to "my high sexual drive," such sexual behaviors are more driven by an antecedent anxiety, the causes of which may be, literally, any conflict — intrapsychic, interpersonal, or environmental. In such cases, as in the case of Andrew, treatment involves not so much identifying the remote developmental antecedents that will stop unwanted sexual behaviors as mastering more appropriate methods for managing the anxieties of the present situation.

One way of conceptualizing the effect of developmental antecedents is as a *learned behavior* that has become problematic. This can be understood as maladaptive from the behaviorist or social learning theoretical perspectives. Whether through the shaping of behavior by its consequences (behaviorist perspective) or through the internalization of social rules and norms (social learning perspective), the individual has learned to do a specific behavior that is now problematic.

■ Megan was physically abused by both parents and by her stepfather when her mother remarried. To protect herself from these beatings, she would withdraw socially and attempt to become "invisible." At the time, the strategy was adaptive and reduced the number of times she was physically abused. Megan "learned" that to avoid physical and emotional trauma, she should be quiet, obedient, and, best of all, invisible.

While this pattern of behavior was protective of her as a child, when she married a rather domineering man, Ronald, whom she thought would protect her, she continued to practice becoming invisible in times of potential disagreement. Her invisibility extended to her sexual intimacy with Ronald. She had no sexual desire for him; she wished to be left alone — and safe. Megan "wanted to desire," to be sexual with Ronald, but she just did not know how. Her adaptive learning of how to avoid physical abuse by her parents was the same maladaptive learning that made her ignorant of how to be intimate with her husband.

Added to the cultural and developmental antecedents, and certainly as a product of these influences, is *the meaning that the individual attaches to the sexual behavior.* For example, the National Health and Social Life Survey found that 31 percent of respondents believed intercourse should occur only within marriage, 44 percent said it should occur only within a loving and caring relationship, and the remaining 25 percent believed intercourse could be used for recreational purposes alone.(10) The data indicate that adults in the United States hold widely divergent attitudes about sexual behavior. Despite a long-standing debate on the role of attitudinal values as antecedents to behavior, it seems, at least at the level of common sense, that most individuals are inclined to behave as they describe their values, or eventually change their attitudes to be consistent with their behavior.

At the individual clinical level, the shades of meaning attributed to sexual behavior become numerous, subtle, and, often, changing. One task of the clinician is to assist the patient to elucidate his or her own attitudinal values about sexual behavior. The process will likely be clarifying for both therapist and patient and will allow them to recognize any significant divergence between attitudes and behaviors or between attitudes held by sexual partners.

In marital and couple therapy, an exploration of attitudinal values about sex can be enlightening. At an appropriate time in the course of therapy, the clinician asks the couple, "Why do you engage in sexual intercourse? Think about this for a moment and then respond." The question and directive require the therapist and couple to pause and think about the answer rather than rush to respond, containing further amplification of the anxiety generated by the question. Thoughtful responses will often reveal not only differences between the partners but also, if one pursues it, complexities within the individuals about their own attitudes. The meanings of sexual intercourse are multiple and frequently discordant: to experience sexual pleasure and release of tension, to have a partner's full attention for a change, to have fun with each other, to be close and intimate, to express love, to act out a (paraphilic) fantasy. But each plays its role as an antecedent of the sexual behavior.

The meanings attributed to compulsive or paraphilic sexual behaviors are more difficult to pursue. Certainly sexual release and pleasure are acknowledged as a motivating factor. Beyond that, however, the meanings of why a man engages in sex with a child or why a woman needs and wants to experience pain and degradation for sexual arousal are often initially hidden from the therapist and from the patient. But meanings are there, and so I return to the case of Andrew, the stockbroker.

■ In about the sixth month of individual therapy, Andrew reported that he was having difficulties with premature ejaculation with his wife. This had happened episodically even before his wife learned about the affair with his staff member. What was remarkable was that he did not experience premature ejaculation in any of his extramarital affairs. The question "why the difference" was obvious grist for the therapeutic mill.

As Andrew came to understand his own responses before and during sexual activity with his wife and with the other women, he said that he feared that his wife didn't really want him inside her. The other women, perhaps aided by his employer status, tended to idealize him (a borderline-personality feature). This idealization replaced his deep-seated insecurities with a borrowed and hollow ego-strength. His temporary confidence kept his anxiety (and sympathetic nervous system response) under control so that he did not experience premature ejaculation. Later in therapy, when the marriage was addressed and improved, premature ejaculation during intercourse with his wife was no longer a problem.

Meanings attributed to sexual behaviors, then, can be elicited and processed with any theoretical system: cognitive-behavioral, existential, or psychoanalytic. What is key, as is further developed in the discussion of the life story perspective in Chapter 6, is that many possible meanings may be attributed after the fact. From the behavior perspective, what is important therapeutically is to explore with the individual the possible meanings that were actually operative leading up to and during the sexual behavior in question. Behavioral, existential, and psychoanalytic "meanings" may be suggested by the therapist, but it is the task of the patient to discover which of the possible meanings were influential in his or her sexual behavior. The discovery of the meaning is validated by an emotional resonance that is felt deeply by the patient and is marked by a sense of relief that comes with discovery, rather than by cerebral assent to a rationale presented by the therapist.

There is a construct in the assumptive world of meaning that deserves special comment: that of an *overvalued idea*. As noted previously in the distinction between actions and behaviors, all behaviors are directed by the idea of the goal toward which they move. Some behaviors — which tend to be exceptional in duration, frequency, or intensity — are guided by an overvalued idea of their goal. This construct of the overvalued idea was developed by Karl Jaspers, in his *General Psychopathology*. (11) An overvalued idea is an organizing principle around which an individual builds his life and in which he invests considerable affect. It is not a psychotic delusion but an idea that is invested with a great amount of affect and leads to action.

Some examples of overvalued ideas may help. The overvalued idea of (continuously) losing weight and being (extremely) thin guides the bingeing, purging, and excessive exercising of the anorexic. The overvalued idea of destroying an evil enemy guides the suicide/murder terrorist's bombing civilian populations. The overvalued idea of being of the other gender guides the gender dysphoric individual to take cross-gender hormones, surgically remove genitalia and breasts, and assume the role of the other gender. The overvalued idea that a sexual behavior will provide an exceptional amount of pleasure, allow escape from the stresses of the present, and contribute to inflated perceptions of ego gratification guides an individual to sexual behaviors that are abnormal in frequency, duration, or object.

While there are various degrees of intensity of the ideas (or "assumptions," in the lexicon of cognitive-behavioral theorists), overvalued ideas often continue to support and give direction to behaviors that can frequently be dismissed as "impulsive behaviors." It is clinically important to identify and to challenge the overvalued idea that is serving as an antecedent to a problematic sexual behavior.

■ Larry was very unhappy with his marriage. It seemed that whenever he and his wife disagreed on a matter (which was often), he would drive about forty miles to a neighboring city and patronize the strip clubs. While there, he would drink excessively, spend much money on paying the hostesses for lap dancing, and occasionally engage in dangerous sexual practices. When confronted by group therapy members who challenged his behavior, Larry quickly responded, "Considering all the grief my wife gives me, I deserve to have a little harmless fun that makes me feel good. The attention the girls give me does the trick (no pun intended)."

While many factors were driving Larry's behavior, there was at the base one overvalued idea: that his sexual behaviors were his compensatory right for all he endured with his wife. The idea was ego-syntonic, and at this point Larry had consciously organized his life around this behavior, despite the risks of disease and of driving under the influence of alcohol.

Larry believed at the beginning of therapy that his trips were deserved and were central to shoring up his sense of self, which was impoverished in general and, as was quite obvious even to him, in his relationship with his wife. For treatment to progress and this behavior to stop, Larry would have to relativize this overvalued idea by examining all the antecedents and consequences connected with the behavior. As one of the antecedents, the overvalued idea had to be challenged to show that the behavior could in no way accomplish all the benefits with which Larry had endowed it. In fact, if he were to look more critically at the behavior, he would learn that it eroded most of the goals he wanted to set for himself.

An overvalued idea is relativized when it is contrasted with other values that the person holds and wishes to express. Practically speaking, this is done by consistent "reality testing," most effectively accomplished in a group of peers that can be at once supportive and challenging. This can also be done by a therapist in individual therapy, but as is familiar to those who work therapeutically with individuals who tend to be motivated by overvalued ideas (e.g., patients with eating disorders and gender identity disorders), the task of such challenging of the overvalued idea often means risking disruption of the therapeutic alliance itself. For this reason, a sexual behavior that has as an antecedent an overvalued idea is best addressed in group therapy. I will say more about group therapy in the next chapter.

Disease and Dimensional Antecedents
While it remains true that individuals have behavioral problems not because of what they have but because of what they do, predisposing and comorbid features can contribute to the expression of the behavior. Brain damage, low intelligence, compulsive traits, and affective illness all can facilitate the expression of the problematic behavior. In saying this, we have invited the disease and dimension perspectives to elaborate on the conditions and traits that each perspective is sensitive to. Thus, while we have started in the behavior perspective, we can and should shift our focus to two other perspectives in order to comprehend the behavior in a way that will facilitate treatment. As I describe more fully in Chapter 7, using the perspectives approach in sexual disorders involves a frequent shifting from one perspective to another in order to understand the full extent of the disorder and to develop an appropriate treatment plan.

THE SEXUAL BEHAVIOR ITSELF
Much effort can be spent in looking into the antecedents (both remote and proximate) of sexual behaviors and hypothesizing about their possible effects on present behaviors. It is certainly necessary work if any treatment is to succeed, because the antecedents will have to be modified

or avoided in order to control or stop the behavior in question. What we must not overlook, however, is the behavior itself. This may seem to be a truism, but it is necessary to repeat: the sexual behavior itself must not be overlooked. The behavior should be quantified in terms of object, frequency, duration, and intensity.

A natural reluctance to talk about sexual behaviors is rooted deeply in our culture. The clinician, although trained to ask sexual questions, is not outside that culture. When this reluctance meets with the patient's shame and embarrassment — not to mention a conscious strategy to obfuscate and deny — then the stage is set for a broad, nonspecific description of the behaviors and multiple assumptions about "what happens" or usually, in a forensic matter, "what happened." This is not sufficient. A clear quantification of the behaviors is necessary for treatment to proceed. The therapist, therapy group, and patient cannot change a behavior when they do not share a consistent appreciation of the manner in which the behavior is expressed. To do this, one must be exact in quantifying the object, frequency, duration, and intensity of the problematic behavior.

Object

The object of the sexual behavior is that which is sexually arousing to the individual. For most adults, the object is an age-appropriate consenting adult. For others, however, the object of sexual arousal can be almost anything. The object may be an inanimate article (e.g., a shoe fetish). It may be a person doing an activity (e.g., a woman undressing without knowing she is being observed). It may be an individual of specific age range and gender (e.g., a prepubescent boy). Or a sexual object may entail fantasizing about or participating in an elaborate dramatized activity (e.g., being humiliated and degraded by another). Some people have multiple objects (e.g., a shoe fetish and an adult consenting partner). Those whose primary if not exclusive sexual objects are other than consenting adults are usually impaired in their ability to develop committed and caring sexual relationships with partners.

Frequency

The frequency of the sexual behavior is just that: how many times the behavior occurs within a specific time period. The challenge of determining the frequency of the sexual behavior lies in not settling for "about" or guesstimate ranges. Reporting the frequency of a behavior during the past thirty days is about as far back as one would normally expect reliable reporting, because of memory distortions and limitations. In sexual behaviors, one must also include in the count the frequency of "attempts" at the behavior that did not result in the behavior itself. For example, the voyeur who went walking through his neighborhood at night but did not see any possible opportunity for peering into a window. This counts as the behavior itself. Last, one should count total orgasms during the period, even if the orgasms were not connected with the sexual behavior in question. The clinician should, however, note the circumstances in which these other orgasms occurred.

Duration

The duration of the sexual activity does not primarily refer to how long the behavior has been occurring in the life of the individual—although this should certainly be ascertained in the sexual history—but to how long the sexual activity takes to perform, from first desire/arousal to completion of the activity. This ranges from a clearly impulsive reaction to a stimulus (e.g., stopping at an erotic massage parlor without intention beforehand) to an elaborate seduction of a vulnerable child that may take months to accomplish. In many paraphilic sexual behaviors and in sexual activity using the Internet, quantifying the time spent in each behavior and the cumulative amount of time may make it clear that, like frequency, duration can have a detrimental effect on the individual's social, relational, and occupational functioning.

Intensity

The intensity of the sexual behavior refers to both the psychological involvement and the sexual and orgasmic pleasure experienced. It is the most difficult of the behavioral markers to quantify and ultimately rests on the quality of the patient's description and the clinician's judgment. Psychological involvement may be in the "here and now" with the partner or may be focused on a fantasy that is the fruit of the individual's own cognition. It may be a blend of both. Orgasmic pleasure includes a slight alteration of consciousness that can contribute to the psychological involvement and therefore the intensity of the behavior. In some sexual behaviors, especially the paraphilic behaviors, the role of orgasm may be relatively minor, and the alteration in consciousness may be greater during the preorgasmic role playing. Individuals will speak of "being in a zone" or "on automatic pilot" to describe their state of mind while engaging in the preorgasmic stages of the sexual behavior. This does not remove individuals' responsibility for initiating the behavior, but it does serve their distortion, if not denial, of the negative consequences of their behaviors.

It may seem at first thought that asking for the information necessary to quantify the object, frequency, duration, and intensity of a sexual behavior will only serve to reinforce the behavior itself. For some patients, supplying the behavior markers may serve as a vehicle of auto-erotic stimulation. If the therapist calls attention to the arousal, it can usually be diffused in the light of therapeutic processing. If, on the other hand, in supplying the information about the specifics of the behavior the patient acquires an affect of eroticized braggadocio, then conditions such as bipolar disorder or antisocial personality disorder should be entertained as possible diagnoses. For most patients, however, supplying the behavioral quantification of the problematic sexual behaviors serves as the first step in gaining mastery over the behaviors. The elaboration of behavior and sharing it with others in the light of day tends to reduce the power of once secret behaviors. Putting words on the behaviors, naming them, usually gives control over them, just as Adam's naming the creatures of the land, sea, and air gave him mastery over them in the Book of Genesis.

CONSEQUENCES OF SEXUAL BEHAVIORS

What happens in sex is not simply sex. The consequences are numerous, positive and negative, and occur in all areas of life: health, relationships, occupation, and sense of self. It is central to any behavioral understanding of sexual activity, therefore, to enumerate the multiple consequences of sexual behaviors, especially those that have developed into a problematic pattern.

Some of the consequences reinforce the behavior, exerting an influence that predisposes the individual to repeat the behavior. Increased sense of self-worth and gender identity, sensual and orgasmic pleasure, and the experience of creating the same results for one's partner are examples of consequences that become the antecedents of subsequent sexual experiences. The sexual behavior will probably be repeated based on the positive or reinforcing consequences that the individual attributes to the behavior. Other possible consequences — sexually transmitted disease, loss of spouse and family, loss of job, incarceration — if the individuals is made conscious of them, will serve to inhibit the sexual behavior.

The "consequential antecedents" of future sexual behaviors — those consequences that become the antecedents of subsequent behaviors —

may be based in reality, such as intimate love between two caring partners, or they may be the embellished product of fantasy. For example,
the sense of self and mastery that is experienced by a man who hires a
prostitute and then sadistically terrorizes her during sex is not based in
reality. The terror and the sadism are real, but the ego inflation that is
gratifying to him is not the product of developmental maturity in interpersonal relationships. It is the fruit of paraphilic and antisocial deception—deception of the tragic prostitute and ultimately deception of
himself.

In a lighter vein, the *New Yorker* cartoon that shows a dog working at
a computer keyboard, with the caption, "On the Internet, nobody
knows you're a dog," captures the deception of self and others that occurs in sexual chat rooms on the Internet. In chat rooms, participants become sexually aroused by the sexual fantasy their activity fosters, rather
than by a real-life encounter with another human being with all his or
her physical and emotional limitations.

It would be a mistake, however, to think of sexual fantasy as "not real"
and therefore not a powerful consequence and antecedent of sexual behavior. Sexual fantasy is as real as imagination and cognition are real. As
such, it is very much a determinant of future sexual behavior. The distinction between reality-based and fantasy-based consequences is that the
former occur in the interpersonal life of the individual while the latter
occur primarily in the head of the individual. It is the task of therapy to
repeatedly delineate this distinction. The individual who is blurring the
distinction will resist mightily, because to admit the difference is to
"lose" the ego-gratifying consequences of the fantasy-informed behavior.

The more an individual judges his or her sexual behavior to be an isolated activity, without consequences other than the sex itself, the more it
can become a major player in the shaping of the person's way of living.
Typically such an individual judges the sexual activity to be neatly com-
partmentalized from the rest of life. The sexual behavior is "here" and the
rest of life is "there." When the "there" becomes "here," as happens in discovery by spouse or arrest by police, the individual is often retrospec-
tively amazed at his or her own ability to deny the potential consequences of the behavior. The cognitive dissonance between what the
person has done and what he or she espouses to value has been mitigated
by the attempt at compartmentalizing the behavior. It is the work of therapy to break down the walls of erotic compartmentalization. The therapist and group therapy members work to integrate the split-off eroticism

by helping the patient see both the power of the behavior in his or her life and the full range of consequences—reinforcing and inhibiting—of the sexual behavior. As the consequences become more conscious, the individual has more resources to choose whether or not to engage in those antecedent behaviors that will lead to a repeat of the problematic sexual behavior.

SEXUAL DYSFUNCTION AS ABNORMAL ILLNESS BEHAVIOR

There are times when a patient presenting with sexual dysfunction is engaging in abnormal illness behavior, "hysteria" in more psychoanalytic terms. A full treatment of a perspectives approach to hysteria itself has been provided by Phillip Slavney.(12) In both sexual and nonsexual abnormal illness behavior, the somatic complaint is an expression of psychological conflicts that the individual either cannot access consciously or chooses to avoid. Two common sexual complaints that may indicate abnormal illness behavior are concern about the appearance of one's genitals and pain with sexual activity.

■ Allan's presenting complaint on his initial evaluation was erectile dysfunction and periodic premature ejaculation, with coital and precoital ejaculation typically occurring within thirty seconds after arousal. He was treated with a combination of cognitive-behavioral therapy and medication—10 mg of paroxetine—for a period of three months. The erectile dysfunction and the premature ejaculation seemed to be resolved. When the paroxetine was discontinued, the erectile dysfunction did not return and the premature ejaculation resolved to a five-minute orgasmic latency without the use of medication.

However, with these sexual dysfunctions resolved, Allan mentioned what he felt was a more serious problem: his penis was too small to give his girlfriend adequate sexual pleasure. He added that this was her complaint also. Allan was quite insistent at this point that he wanted a referral to a surgeon who specialized in penile augmentation.

For Allan, the *manifestations of abnormal illness behavior* are seen in his serial somatic complaints that he believes are real and portend more serious problems. The erectile and ejaculatory dysfunctions were probably a result of the anxiety he felt about sexual interaction with a very demanding partner. Therapy helped him deal more with the intimate social anxiety of the behavior rather than with more standard sensate focus control skills. The social anxiety was also mitigated by the use of the paroxetine. In many ways, however, it was only symptomatic relief.

The second complaint, inadequate penis size, was more classically hysterical. The somatic problem represented a conflict, which Allan was unable to acknowledge, about the adequacy of his masculinity. The abnormal illness behavior was his seeking attention from health providers for a somatic complaint, for what was at root a psychological problem.

The *personality traits* typically manifested in persons engaging in abnormal illness behavior are preoccupation with oneself (low Agreeableness) and high Neuroticism (especially anxiety).(13) These traits work synergistically to focus the individual—and those who would treat or care for the individual—on the somatic complaint. This focusing on the complaint serves the dual purpose of gaining the attention of supportive others and avoiding the psychological conflict that, ultimately, the individual must face alone.

The circumstances in which abnormal illness behavior occurs are similar to the psychosocial factors that produce depression and frustration in most people. Something adverse is happening in the person's relationships or emotions. In abnormal illness behavior, there is some influence that sustains the behavior and usually some secondary gain from the sick role. In Allan's case, the sustaining—and perhaps the initiating—influence was his girlfriend's belief that his penis was too small. Matters were not going well in the sexual aspect of the relationship. The problem was his small penis—an attribution and belief that was held by the couple. The belief then became an overvalued idea as Allan organized both his distress and his abnormal illness behavior around seeking a surgical remedy. The secondary gain of the illness behavior was his having some temporary "cover" from his girlfriend's dissatisfaction by being able to say that he was doing something about the problem.

The treatment of sexual dysfunction as abnormal illness behavior has two principal elements: (i) do not directly challenge (the falsity of) the presenting symptom; and (ii) invite the patient to use the symptom as a "helpful" sign of some psychological vulnerability that will be present for his or her lifetime

- ■ The treatment for Allan's "small" penis consisted largely in not colluding with his speculation about augmentation surgery. This was accomplished by reinforcing every trace of ambivalence he had about the procedure. He was not referred to a urologist for the purpose of "proving" to him that his penis was of normal size. Such authoritative decree is seldom curative. Instead, the therapist helped Allan critically observe the relationship with his girlfriend: her practice of attributing all sexual problems to his small penis; his inability to assert himself with her, not only sexually but in other dimensions of the relationship. Eventually, after about six months of individual therapy, Allan and his girlfriend entered couple therapy with a different therapist to address the dynamics central to their interactions. They decided to terminate the relationship.

Allan returned for a consultation with his individual therapist and admitted relief at the breakup and what now appeared to him as the foolish idea of penile augmentation. He was advised that both the sexual dysfunction and the fear that his penis was too small could return. He was to take these emotional and sexual signs as invitations to address issues in the relationship and in his own sense of self. While never showing a high degree of psychological insight, Allan did give at least a nodding agreement to these concluding recommendations.

Like penile size in men, painful intercourse, dyspareunia, in women and men may be an expression of abnormal illness behavior. But a caveat is in order here, especially concerning painful intercourse for women. The caveat comes from the disease perspective: many medical conditions, such as vulvodynia, vulvar vestibulitis, and other dermatological conditions, can cause introital pain.(14–16) A thorough examination by a physician who is experienced in diagnosing and treating dyspareunia should be obtained before formulating the dyspareunia as abnormal illness behavior.

SUMMARY

The behavior perspective is concerned with what a person does. When sexual behaviors are the reason for professional assistance either sought voluntarily by the individual or required by a third party, the task of evaluation is to delineate clearly the specifics of the behavior and to elaborate the antecedents and consequences of the behavior. The more complete the knowledge about the ABC of behavior — antecedents, behaviors, consequences — the more effective will be the behavior perspective. The behavior perspective is helpful both for stopping problematic behaviors (e.g., pedophilia) and for starting desired but absent behaviors (e.g., a couple achieving sexual intimacy after fears of dysfunction). The behavior perspective invites the clinician and patient to focus on those conditions that are maintaining expression of the problematic behavior rather than on what may have started the behavior initially. The perspective draws from all dimensions of the biopsychosocial world in its work to identify the antecedents and consequences of a behavior. Therefore, the other three perspectives — disease, dimension, and life story — contribute to implementation of the behavior perspective.

■ 5

TREATMENT OF
SEXUAL DISORDERS
IN THE BEHAVIOR PERSPECTIVE

The behavior perspective is concerned with goal-directed behaviors (see Table 4.1). It examines the antecedents, the behaviors themselves, and the consequences of behaviors. Treatment in the behavior perspective is directed at promoting behaviors that are wanted but do not occur or, conversely, at stopping behaviors that are unwanted yet continue to occur. The former method usually is employed in the treatment of sexual dysfunctions; the latter is used when unwanted sexual disorders such as pedophilia and compulsive sexual behaviors are the target problem. In both instances — starting wanted behaviors and stopping unwanted behaviors — present behaviors must be replaced with new ones that are more appropriate for the desired goal.

This chapter examines the treatment of sexual dysfunctions and disorders from the behavior perspective. I do not intend to provide a detailed treatment manual for sexual dysfunctions and disorders. Several excellent resources are already in print, and the reader will be referred to these for a fuller description of treatment interventions. My goal here is to amplify the information provided in the previous chapter, highlighting treatment issues as they pertain to the behavior perspective.

BEHAVIORAL TREATMENT OF SEXUAL DYSFUNCTION

The classic behavioral treatment of sexual dysfunction is sensate focus therapy. Developed by William Masters and Virginia Johnson in the 1960s, the technique seeks to assist a couple experiencing sexual dysfunction to gradually change their sexual interaction from an anxiety-

and frustration-producing event into one that is relaxed, nonthreatening, and mutually pleasurable.(1) Technically, sensate focus therapy relies on the principle of reciprocal inhibition. Behaviors that are riddled with anxiety are replaced by behaviors that bring relaxation and eventually sexual pleasure to the partners. Gradually, over a period of several weeks, the partners are guided through a nondemanding increase of sensual and then sexual pleasuring behaviors with each other. Abilities to give and receive sensual and sexual pleasure are developed by focusing on the pleasurable effects of touch and other sensual and sexual activities.

In the four decades since the work of Masters and Johnson, sensate focus therapy has been amplified by strategies that are more cognitive and relegate the sensate focus treatment to the role of but one component in the overall treatment.(2–5) Of the treatments for sexual dysfunction that have been empirically validated, treatments of primary anorgasmia in women and erectile dysfunction in men are "well established," while treatments for secondary anorgasmia in women and premature ejaculation in men are "probably efficacious."(6) By and large, these empirically validated treatments are behaviorally based, although with recent augmentation by somatic treatments such as sildenafil and penile injections for male sexual dysfunctions.

In sensate focus therapy, the antecedents of the couple's baseline sexual interaction are examined. Is there privacy? Is the 3-year-old likely to storm through the bedroom door in the midst of congress? How thick are the walls relative to each partner's need for privacy? Are there distractions in the environment? Is the TV on? What if the phone rings? Has either partner something urgent and pressing on his or her mind that needs to be talked about? Does either partner feel a demand to perform sexually? Is fatigue, illness, or menstrual status a problem for either partner? Has too much alcohol been ingested? What is the state of emotional intimacy in the relationship? Is it sufficient for sexual interaction for both partners? All these and other antecedents, uncovered by a careful examination of the life of the couple, are either positive or negative factors in promoting the desired behavior.

The sexual behaviors themselves must be conscientiously observed and described in the therapy session. Is there a period of relaxed touching and "tuning in" on the other, or is there a race for orgasm? What are the touches and caresses that are pleasurable to each, and do they occur? Do the partners ask each other for those touches that are pleasurable? Conversely, are they able to tell each other that a particular touch is not pleasurable or erotic? Are they open to different sexual scripts, that is, different patterns of interacting with each other? How much time is spent in foreplay? How much time is spent in close contact after orgasm has been achieved? What if one or both partners do not achieve orgasm? How does each react to the absence of orgasm, verbally and emotionally? Elaborating on such questions from the therapist may not be easy, but the partners will be rewarded by developing better communication and sexual skills if they do so. In a more classical sensate focus treatment, discussion of any nonsexual topic in therapy is generally seen as a diversion from the primary work. Such diversion from examining the sexual behaviors is often considered a collusion between patients and therapist that serves to avoid the embarrassment and anxiety the sexual content provokes.

Last, sensate focus therapy as a behavioral treatment is concerned with the consequences of the sexual interaction. As noted in Chapter 4, the consequences of one behavior become the antecedents of the subsequent behavior. The principal consequences of sexual behavior are the quality of sexual satisfaction, the emotional relatedness of the couple, and the sense of self that emerges from the sexual interaction. Sexual satisfaction should include sensual pleasure as well as sexual excitement and orgasm. How does each partner describe his or her own level of sexual satisfaction? It may be surprising, for example, for one partner to learn that the other partner may not desire orgasm. Emotional relatedness occurs both during sexual intercourse and in the hours or days that follow. Is each partner aware of the sense of relatedness the other experiences? Is this different for each and different at various times? And how do the partners feel about themselves as man, woman, partner, spouse, lover after the sexual interaction? As with all the other consequences, this sense of self is what is carried into the next sexual interaction with the partner.

Sensate focus therapy is, therefore, the primary behavioral treatment of sexual dysfunction that essentially involves the antecedents, behaviors, and consequences of the couple's sexual life. Its goal of improving the quality of their interactions employs traditional methods of behavioral therapy: observation, behavioral goal setting, and contingency management. In its evolution from the initial design of Masters and Johnson, it has developed into a behavioral component that works with treatments from other perspectives, as described in Chapter 7.

BEHAVIORAL TREATMENT OF SEXUAL DISORDERS

If the typical behavioral goal of the treatment of sexual dysfunction is to facilitate a behavior, the behavioral treatment of sexual disorders is to stop an unwanted sexual behavior or limit it to certain circumstances that are less injurious or problematic. Four behavioral characteristics of sexual disorders may, and frequently do, overlap: (i) driven, compulsive sexual behaviors (e.g., the man who two or three times a week exposes himself to women); (ii) impulsive sexual behaviors (e.g., the individual who responds to sexual stimuli without any deliberation); (iii) paraphilic sexual behaviors (e.g., the individual who is attracted sexually to children); and (iv) sexual behaviors that are neither driven nor paraphilic but are harmful to self or others in their possible consequences (e.g., the woman who engages in weekly sexual encounters with strangers and without protection from sexually transmitted diseases).

Compulsive sexual behaviors are noted for their frequency and almost routine, automatic pattern. They are behaviors that have been routinized by their habitual expression. In some instances, the individual with compulsive sexual behaviors describes being "on automatic pilot" as he goes through the patterned behavior. There may even be a sense of anhedonia, or lack of pleasurable involvement in the sexual behavior.

Impulsive sexual behaviors are marked by spontaneity, and to a certain degree by the intensity of the behaviors. Gerald Moeller and his associates have offered a construct of impulsivity that consists of three elements: (i) decreased sensitivity to *negative* consequences of behavior; (ii) rapid, unplanned reactions to stimuli before complete processing of information; and (iii) lack of regard for long-term consequences of the behavior.(7) Most of the research on impulsivity has focused on aggression. However, Moeller's threefold definition matches well the clinical characteristics of individuals with impulsive sexual behavior.

Survey data are available on consenting adult sexual interactions and adult masturbation,(8) but there are no epidemiological studies on the frequency of other types of sexual behaviors (e.g., use of the Internet for erotic purposes) that would enable the clinician to say that the amount of behavior for an individual is statistically normal in frequency. In these instances, it is up to the clinician and the patient to determine whether the frequency of the sexual behavior is such that it interferes with the patient's occupational, social, or relational goals and values. For example, a man who surfs the Internet for erotic sites ten hours a week while at work has a frequency and duration that is compromising his production at work. As mentioned in Chapter 4, in addition to high frequency, the driven quality of the behavior, its intensity, is often evident when the individual reports some variant of compulsivity once the behavior has begun. While there may be some attempt to escape responsibility for the behavior by referring to the "automatic pilot" or semidissociative state, if reported consistently enough it is a reliable indicator that the ego-control of the behavior is being eroded by subjective forces generically referred to as "motivating drives."

Paraphilic behaviors are typified by their object, that is, by the target of their erotic attraction or by the enacting of a sexual fantasy in sexual behavior. The paraphilic target is an inanimate object (e.g., an undergarment), a partial (human) object (e.g., a foot), or an unsuspecting or nonconsenting person (as in exhibitionism, voyeurism, frotteurism, or pedophilia). In paraphilic sexual behaviors, the individual's sexual fantasy is primary. It can be expressed in masturbation, but since the fantasy and arousal tend to crave the greater stimulation provided by the excitement and risk of being acted out in the external world, the paraphilic fantasy eventually involves a real person, consenting or not.

The third group, those who engage in *nondriven and nonparaphilic but definitely problematic sexual behaviors,* is an especially difficult group to describe, let alone treat. Their behaviors do not have the frequency or the dissociative disinhibition of driven behaviors. They are clearly not paraphilic by the criteria of the DSM-IV-TR. But the behaviors do pose a serious risk to the self or others. Sexually transmitted diseases, loss of family stability, and loss of employment are possible consequences but are often insufficient to modify or stop the sexual behavior. While all three groups of behaviors profit from behavioral treatment intervention, this third group in particular usually requires therapy that relies on information provided by the dimension perspective and strategies provided by the life story perspective. For this group almost more than the other two groups, the issues of decision and personal values and meaning may be the most salient factors in therapy.

Pretreatment: Assessing Motivation

For all three groups, however, *assessment of motivation for change* is the first step in the treatment for stopping unwanted sexual behaviors. In most cases, a third party (e.g., a partner, an employer, the courts) has brought a person with problematic sexual behaviors into treatment. In some cases the individual voluntarily initiates treatment, with no external threat, but these cases are rare. More often that not, the individual with compulsive, paraphilic, or injurious sexual behaviors has been brought to evaluation and treatment by the demands of a third party. It is crucial for determining an individual's resources for treatment, therefore, that the clinician assess his or her motivation for change and report this information to the patient and to the parties requesting the treatment.

One of the most useful triage constructs that has emerged from the addiction treatment field is the Transtheoretical model of James Prochaska and Carlo DiClemente.(9) Their stages-of-change model consists of six stages: precontemplative, contemplative, preparation, action, maintenance, and termination stages. Using this model regarding the behavior in question, the clinician evaluating a patient for treatment assigns the individual to: (i) the *precontemplative stage* (not thinking about stopping or controlling the behavior); (ii) the *contemplative stage* (considering stopping but ambivalent about "losing" the gratifications that the behavior brings); (iii) the *preparation stage* (making adjustments to take action in the next month); or lastly, (iv) the *active stage* (having made a subjective decision and having taken at least one step to stop the unwanted behavior). Granted that motivational states may be difficult to assess, it is nonetheless important that both the individual and the treatment team or therapist have an accurate appraisal of the true motivation for change of the individual. The individual should be assisted to progress to the active stage, if necessary using the threat of loss of relationship or incarceration, so that the treatment then can effectively begin.

As stated in Chapter 4, treatment from the behavior perspective assumes that, at some rudimentary level, in every behavior the individual is choosing to act. In controlling and stopping unwanted sexual behaviors, the ability to behave consistently with verbalized (and in some cases believed) intentions may be compromised by habit, attitude, and physiological dependence. Nevertheless, the individual must make a decision to stop the unwanted sexual behaviors. Without this active stage of decision and action, no successful treatment of sexual disorders can be achieved, regardless of the duration of treatment or the reputation of the treating facility or provider.

Treatment Stage One: Identifying and Controlling the Antecedents
The circumstances that initially caused a behavior to occur are usually not the conditions that promote its maintenance and continuation.

■ As a young boy, Rob was dressed as a girl one Halloween by his older sister, and as he made his door-to-door trick-or-treat journey, he was praised by his mother and neighbors for "what a good girl he would have made." The initial Halloween cross-dressing was not sexually exciting but it was ego-gratifying. Subsequently, as a young boy, Rob cross-dressed in order to repeat the ego gratification. He would admire himself in the mirror. When he became pubescent, the cross-dressing became eroticized and he would become sexually aroused and masturbate.

Now in his early thirties, Rob reported cross-dressing both for sexual excitement and release as well as for relaxation. His wife had discovered the behavior and was afraid for the sexual safety of their children, and she had threatened to leave the marriage. This threat brought Rob into treatment with an ambivalent request to help him stop the behavior.

Clearly, the factors that started the behavior of cross-dressing on Halloween twenty-five years ago are not the factors that reinforce and maintain the current cross-dressing behavior. While it might be interesting and intellectually satisfying for Rob to remember that first cross-dressing incident and his emotional reaction to it, that recollection and insight will do little to stop the present goal-directed behavior of cross-dressing, looking at himself in a mirror, becoming sexually excited, and masturbating to the vision of himself as a woman.

If the behavior is to be stopped, the antecedents that are effective in maintaining Rob's practice of cross-dressing today must be altered. The antecedents are all those factors that proximately precede the behavior: physiological drives, behaviors, and acquired influences, both internal (e.g., drugs, beliefs, attitudes) and external (e.g., environment, relationships). A subset of antecedents can be considered "triggers," circumstances that immediately precede the behavior.

■ Rob's antecedents were any set of circumstances that challenged his sense of worth. His supervisor putting pressure on him at work, the children disobeying him, but especially his wife criticizing or disagreeing with him caused him to feel both demoralized and anxious. He had the assumptive belief that his cross-dressing in secret was his "little island of repose," and he would strategize about how to arrange for the necessary privacy. When his wife left the house for an extended period of time with the children, the "trigger" was there. Rob would unpack his hidden stash of female clothing and engage in the cross-dressing behavior. Except for the last incident, he was able to return the clothing and, with some shame, resume his day "as if nothing happened." During the last cross-dressing episode, his wife unexpectedly returned home earlier than planned and caught him in the midst of his cross-dressing ritual.

Applying Prochaska and DiClemente's motivation-for-change model, we see that Rob was between the contemplative and action stages of behavior change. He wanted to stop the behavior and had cooperated fully with the evaluation. Altering the antecedents of the cross-dressing behavior would involve Rob's stopping some behaviors as well as developing others. He should remove the stash of clothing. To manage the identified trigger, Rob should have a plan for activities when alone. It may initially be necessary to leave the house when his wife does (e.g., work in the yard, run errands). Psychologically, Rob has to develop an internal vision of himself as a more competent employee, parent, and spouse and must be able to assert himself in life situations as a more competent person. He and his wife may need marital therapy to adjust to the personal changes that Rob must make in terms of assertiveness.

Treatment Stage Two: Stopping the Behavior

Unlike other compulsive behaviors, such as alcohol or drug abuse, which commonly occur in social settings, compulsive or paraphilic sexual behaviors often have a massive wall of secrecy around them. The behaviors have for years been practiced in secret, out of shame or fear of arrest and incarceration. One of the initial steps is to destroy this protective wall of secrecy.

Eroding the wall of shame and secrecy can be accomplished by inviting the individual, now a patient in therapy, to explain the behavior in minute detail, describing the external circumstances, the behaviors themselves, and the internal responses and fantasies. If initially the recounting becomes sexually exciting for the patient, this sexual response should be remarked on and processed in the therapy. Arousal may occur if the patient is allowed to "hide" in the semidissociative state of the behaviors rather than recounting the behaviors in the real-life circumstance of the individual or group therapy session. For the most part, however, repeated elaboration will have the effect of providing a realistic appraisal of the behavior as a pattern that is a maladaptive effort to respond to subjective and objective antecedents. It will, in some cases, assist the patient to see the effects of the behavior on the lives of others, including, as in Rob's case, his loved ones. It can open the door for the development of empathy.

Group therapy is the preferred treatment modality for stopping unwanted behaviors, including unwanted sexual behaviors. Both the twelve-step programs modeled on AA and behaviorally focused group therapy accomplish the twofold task of challenge and support. Members are challenged primarily by other group members to "get with the program" or stop deceiving themselves about the antecedents of the behaviors. The AA saying, "It takes one to know one," applies to those who are struggling with unwanted sexual behaviors. Denial, rationalization, deception are sooner or later labeled as such in a group setting far more effectively than in individual therapy.

In addition to challenge, groups also provide support for individuals who are trying to change deeply ingrained behaviors. Sponsors or group therapy members who have reached some level of control over their behaviors offer role models for the new members. Words of encouragement after a relapse or of praise after an achievement help the individual to progress in his or her program to stop the behaviors. Last, but perhaps most important, are the unspecific curative factors in any group process. Through engagement in the group as a microcosm of the human community, an individual is given the opportunity to become more deeply human. In most group processes, therefore, the unwanted sexual behaviors are viewed as obstacles to this process of becoming a fuller and more effective human being.

For those who are able to understand themselves in terms of their own psychosocial history and the role of this history in their behavior and attitudes, individual therapy that addresses the life story may be helpful in preventing relapse. It may serve also as an effective complementary treatment to group therapy. However, individual therapy, especially insight-oriented therapy, is not recommended as the sole modality to stop unwanted sexual behavior. Even for the psychologically minded patient, insight into the putative causes of the behavior and emotional cathexis to the insight or memory are often not sufficient to stop the behavior. For those who have difficulty in understanding themselves psychologically, stressing an insight-oriented treatment will not be successful in stopping the behavior. It may worsen it by providing the opportunity for another "failure" at correction, thus increasing the frustration of patient and therapist alike. This delivers the message to the individual that he or she is not able to stop the behavior, even with the help of psychological experts. Individual therapy, insight-oriented or cognitive-behavioral, should be used as an adjunct to the primary modality of group therapy to stop unwanted behaviors.

Medication for Behaviors

Pharmacological interventions may be necessary for some individuals to gain control of their sexual behaviors.(10) In terms of the perspectives, the use of medication in the treatment of behavioral disorders employs the disease perspective. This is not to say that a disease process is occurring in the individual with a compulsive or paraphilic disorder, but rather that the clinician and patient have elected to control sexual behaviors by modifying the body's physiological functions. This is a reminder that the use of the perspectives in therapy is not a disjunctive process in which it is *either* this perspective *or* that perspective. Treatment using the perspectives methodology is conjunctive: using this perspective *and* that perspective. It is a selection of one perspective as the primary treatment modality, then the integration of the other perspectives as appropriate for the understanding and treatment of the particular case.

Pharmacological treatment should be considered when any of the following conditions exist: (i) there is a clear and present danger that others may become the victims of sexual violence, as in pedophilia and sexual sadism; (ii) behavioral methods have proven unsuccessful when used independently; (iii) the sexual behaviors are excessively driven, as measured by their frequency, duration, intensity, and lack of attention to consequences; (iv) a comorbid condition (e.g., depression, bipolar disorder, dementia) is augmenting the expression of the sexual behavior.

Unless the behavior's frequency and intensity indicate the need for an antiandrogen medication, the first line of pharmacological treatment is the use of selective serotonin reuptake inhibitor (SSRI) medications.(11) The advantages of these medications are that they can treat an affective disorder (even subclinical in its symptom level) and that their secondary effects of reducing sexual drive and obsessions with sexual content are positive effects in treating the sexual disorder. The disadvantages are that the SSRIs may not be potent enough to counter the physiological components of the sexual behavior or that the common side effect of anorgasmia may contribute to the patient's noncompliance.

The second-line pharmacological treatment is the use of medications that have an antiandrogen effect. In both men and women, the injection or ingestion of substances such as medroxyprogesterone acetate, cyproterone acetate, and depot leuprolide acetate lowers the testosterone levels and through this mechanism greatly reduces sexual drive without necessarily making the individual unable to have sexual intercourse.(12–14) With the diminished drive and reduced preoccupation with the unwanted sexual behavior, the individual is able to employ the strategies developed in the behavioral treatment. The advantage of the antiandrogens is their powerful effect on decreasing libido. The disadvantage is that there may be medical effects such as reduced bone density, weight gain, and feminization. Regular monitoring of bone density, glucose levels, and liver function tests is advised in cases of chronic use.

Other medications have been and undoubtedly will be used as adjuncts for controlling behavioral problems. Paul Federoff reported a case in which he was treating a man for anxiety disorder.(15) The patient also cross-dressed, although this was not the object of treatment. To treat the anxiety, Federoff prescribed buspirone, an antianxiety medication. The patient reported that after a few weeks his anxiety was reduced and that, strangely, he had not felt the urge to cross-dress. When the medication was stopped, both the anxiety and the cross-dressing behaviors returned. When resumed, the medication again had the effect of reducing the anxiety and, without intending it, stopping the urge to cross-dress. In another case report, naltrexone, an opioid agonist, was used in the successful treatment of a man who had been engaged in kleptomania and compulsive sexual behaviors.(16) The naltrexone controlled both behaviors and, when stopped, the behaviors returned. For individuals with dementia, neuroleptics have been used to manage sexual behaviors that are nonresponsive to behavioral treatments and remain disruptive to residential living.(17)

Thus, medications such as SSRIs, antiandrogens, antianxiety drugs, or neuroleptics are used to control problematic sexual behaviors. In the perspectives methodology, the employment of such medications is the welcome integration of the disease perspective with behavior perspective treatment.

Relapse Prevention: Monitoring and Managing the Consequences

No behavioral treatment program for a sexual disorder consisting of unwanted sexual behaviors is complete without a relapse-prevention component. The model here is the AA "recovering alcoholic" who lives "one day at a time." Individuals with a compulsive sexual disorder or a paraphilic pattern of sexual arousal are well served if they view themselves as persons who will always be inclined to that particular expression of sexual behavior. In terms of the perspectives, they should work daily to control the behavior rather than assume they are cured of disease.

The first element in a relapse-prevention program is the ability to *identify the "trigger" circumstances* of the unwanted sexual behavior and to take steps to avoid or ameliorate them. To do this, the individual must have or must develop in treatment a self-monitoring vigilance and an ability to be critical of his or her behaviors and assumptions. A special trigger today is use of the Internet. If individuals use the Internet to engage in forms of unwanted sexual behavior, they have already pulled the "trigger" and returned to the pattern that brought them into treatment in the first place.

The second element in relapse prevention is *regular consultation* with a clinician who can assist the individual in observing and managing the consequences of his or her behaviors. The frequency of these consultations may range from monthly, immediately following the initial treatment, to annually, when both patient and clinician see the tension and risk for expressing the behaviors as low. The consultations should be scheduled at an agreed-upon frequency and address at least three topics: (i) assessment of how the "triggers" are being managed; (ii) assessment of whether the replacement behaviors (e.g., relationship with spouse) are being developed; and (iii) completion of a mental status examination. In some cases where there is risk of harm to others or incarceration, a polygraph evaluation can ascertain whether any of the problematic behaviors have occurred since the previous consultation. For patients whose regimen includes antiandrogen medication, compliance can be assessed by checking testosterone levels. Any concerns that arise from these three points indicate a need for more frequent consultation or the resumption of regular therapy.

There are several forms of the twelve-step program, as originated in AA: Sexaholics Anonymous, Sex and Love Addicts Anonymous, and other variants. In general, these organizations support participants in their work of avoiding unwanted sexual behaviors. As locally directed, nonprofessionally led groups, they vary in their effectiveness. Before making a referral to a particular group, the clinician should inquire about how it is organized, what its rules are, and what its position is on therapy for its members. In practice, this information can be obtained by listening to new patients who have participated in these groups.

Relapse prevention is also a component in the treatment of sexual dysfunction. In these cases, the individual is trying to initiate and maintain a wanted sexual behavior. Relapse from successful treatment occurs when the behavior is again absent or dysfunctional. A bit of common-sense advice for couples who have successfully completed a course of sexual therapy is that they should expect the dysfunction to appear again in the future. They are vulnerable to sexual dysfunction. They should take the reappearance of the dysfunction not as a sign of failure but as an invitation to review the conditions that, as they have learned in their therapy, are the likely causes. The partners then can directly address the conditions (e.g., general communication lags) and their sexual life with the methods learned in their sensate focus therapy.

ETHICAL CONSIDERATIONS

Therapeutic efforts either to stop unwanted sexual behaviors or to start wanted sexual behaviors should raise ethical questions — for individuals in treatment, clinicians, and ultimately society as a whole. While sexual behaviors are vehicles for some of the most exquisite of life's pleasures and intimate joys, they also account for a considerable amount of pain, suffering, and violence inflicted by some individuals on others. The legal, religious, and cultural institutions of a society have a vested interest in providing norms for sexual behaviors. The norms promote the society's stability and preserve the values treasured by the particular institutions. How this is done, especially in the context of Western culture that treasures individualism and unfettered free choice, is the nub of the ethical debate on sexual behaviors.

The subtleties of this question cannot be addressed in any detail here. What I can suggest is that the discussion of ethical considerations of sexual behaviors be framed in the context of the dialectic of social constructionism versus essentialism.(18) In brief, social constructionism posits that all behaviors have meanings and values constructed and attributed to them by the context of the culture in which they operate. Essentialism holds that there is an innate order, or ontology, in the human system that is the source of values attributed to behaviors. In general, social constructionism is a value-relative system; essentialism is a value-absolute system. In sexual behaviors, social constructionism speaks of varieties of sexual behavior that are chosen by individuals, while essentialism sees some sexual behaviors as positive or good and others as negative or bad, depending on whether or not they are consistent with the vision of the good society that the essentialism holds. I will have more to say about essentialism and social constructionism in Chapter 6, on the life story perspective.

The primary ethical considerations in working with the behavior perspective are twofold: (i) the clinician and patient should be aware of their own positioning in the social constructionist versus essentialist continuum; and (ii) from this basis, the two should agree on a treatment contract that does violence to neither party's values. In practice, this requires the clinician, in his or her own mind, to frame the goal of the behavioral treatment as promoting sexual behaviors that (i) both clinician and patient (or patients) value positively (e.g., intercourse between a happily married couple); or (ii) the clinician values positively for others but not for himself or herself, and can assist others who do value such behaviors to express (e.g., same-sex sexual intimacies); and (iii) the clinician values negatively and does not want to assist in an individual who values the behaviors (e.g., behaviors involving infliction of pain on nonconsenting partners or vulnerable persons such as minors).

While the first and third situations are relatively straightforward, the second situation poses the greatest ethical challenge for the clinician. The challenge often involves walking with the patient down a path of erotic expression that the clinician would never choose but which he or she has judged to be a valid and meaningful path for the patient. This experience can often give the clinician a broadening view of the human condition that is enriching. It can also be a self-deception under the influence of financial reward, voyeurism, or increased self-esteem about being a highly tolerant clinician. Prevention of such self-deception is possible through a healthy review of one's motivation, conducted alone or with a trusted colleague. It serves the welfare of neither the clinician nor the patient if the two enter a behavioral program marked by a high degree of ambivalence on both sides about the value of the behavioral goal. Values, like sex, eventually will out.

SUMMARY

Treatment in the behavior perspective aims at stopping unwanted sexual behaviors or starting wanted sexual behaviors. To accomplish this, the antecedents of the behavior, the behavior itself, and the consequences of the behavior are the main foci of treatment. The common modalities of treatment are couple therapy to start successful sexual behaviors and group therapy to stop unwanted sexual behaviors. Adjunctive interventions such as antiandrogen medication for sexual disorders and prosexual medications for sexual dysfunction are examples of using the disease perspective with the behavior perspective as base. Similarly, adjunctive individual therapy that explores issues of value and meaning is an example of the complementary use of the life story perspective. In all treatment involving sexual behaviors, the clinician should have a clear understanding of the ethical positions that guide his or her work with the individuals seeking assistance.

SEX AND THE
LIFE STORY PERSPECTIVE:
THE QUESTION OF MEANING

Birth, sexual bonding, and death are human experiences that cultures, religions, and societies invest with profound meaning, and they protect that meaning with rituals, ceremonies, and laws. Epics and epic heroes emerge from the collective unconscious of nations. Nations wage wars to protect meanings and values. Individuals seek to share in the narratives of their "own kind" by understanding the narrative of their lives as both connected to and unique within the greater community. This is what gives meaning and direction to people's lives.

Given the several roles of sexual behavior—pleasure, bonding, reproduction—in the life of the individual within his or her community, several meanings can be assigned to these behaviors. In the complexity of these meanings and the varied challenges they create, an individual's understanding of the meaning of sexual behavior and the relational context it typically requires can become distorted or confused. We look to the life story perspective to address the question of sex and meaning.

AN OVERVIEW OF THE LIFE STORY PERSPECTIVE

The life story perspective relies on narrative as the logic for understanding the clinical data presented by an individual (see Table 6.1). The narrative finds cohesion and developmental sequence in any well-developed

TABLE 6.1

*An Overview of the Life Story Perspective in the Context
of the Other Three Perspectives*

Perspective	Logic	What the Patient _____	Treatment
Disease	Categories	Has.	Alleviate or cure
Dimension	Gradation and quantification	Is.	Assist in adaptation and response
Behavior	Goal directed, teleological	Does.	Interrupt, replace behaviors
Life story	**Narrative**	**Encounters and gives meaning to.**	**Reinterpret or reconstruct narrative**

Source: McHugh PR. Managed care and the four perspectives. Paper presented at Academic Behavioral Healthcare Consortium, June 15, 2001.

theory or myth — Freudian, Jungian, Adlerian, or North American Indian. Whatever its heuristic structure, the narrative gives direction, cohesion, and meaning to the individual's life journey. It says that this path, with all its vagaries, trials, and tribulations, is the path the person has trodden and that this life narrative is what it is today because of what he or she has both endured and created. The life story perspective rejects the notion that the human life is merely a random event and that chaos is the only "unifying" construct.

In encounters with persons and participation in events, individuals generate a narrative that provides meaning for themselves and, in most cases, for the society in which they live. Sometimes the structure of the narrative gets lost, is forgotten, or becomes meaningless for the individual. At such times a crisis generally ensues. For most persons this crisis, or decision point in life, contains both peril and promise. Relying on friends, family, and internal resources, the individual strives to reconstruct the narrative or, if necessary, to create a new one. But at times of such crisis, the individual may also seek out the assistance of a professional "narrative maker," the psychotherapist. Together, they attempt to understand the past and to develop a narrative that gives the patient future direction.

A question immediately arises here: which narrative is the right one? Is it a narrative emerging from the theory in which the therapist has been schooled and has invested years of professional and personal effort? Or is it the narrative of the ethnic, cultural, or religious group in which the patient has grown up or with which he or she identifies? Does the narrative give a causal explanation of the individual's present state? Does it lend understanding to the present such that it "makes sense" or even "has meaning"?

The life story perspective addresses these questions and, in so doing, affirms the therapeutic necessity of a cohesive narrative that generates meaning for the individual. It affirms that humans are more than the diseases they have, more than their traits and abilities, more than the behaviors they have performed or omitted. The life story perspective states that to understand the person who happens to be the patient, both therapist and patient must collaborate in the task of creating or remembering the narrative, story, and myth that provide understanding and meaning to the patient's life journey.

The form elements of creating a narrative are setting, sequence, and outcome. The social and emotional setting in which events occurred, the sequence in which they occurred, the outcomes that flowed from the events, and the individual's perception of the events are the core elements of therapy in the life story perspective. In this perspective, therapy is a psychohistorical work and contains within it the same limitations that historians have always struggled with: historical bias and contrived causation.

Historical bias can occur in the choice of what is remembered and amplified in therapy. The patient and the therapist can collude to focus on certain events and ignore others. For the patient, this may be an attempt to avoid painful emotions. For the therapist, it may be an attempt to reinforce consistency in a theoretical system rather than explore an event or reaction that may challenge the application of such theory. *Contrived causation* is the tendency to read causality as a direct and single effect of one event on another: "Your inability to have an orgasm results from that event at age 5 when your mother caught you masturbating." While this may seem exaggerated when set in bold relief, the tendency to contrived causation is subtle and widespread in the practice of those who use the life story perspective exclusively and uncritically. The most recent example of this is the fabrication of memories of sexual abuse, the product of overzealous and theoretically narrow therapists rather than the recall of tragic events.

Although historical bias and contrived causation can compromise the validity of the life story perspective, the perspective should not be jettisoned as a therapeutic method. What is needed is a complex reading of the narrative that allows for multifactorial influences, including insights provided by the disease, dimension, and behavior perspectives. Without the life story perspective, interventions through the other three perspectives may be technically efficient but lacking in recognition of the unique person who is the patient.

THE PSYCHOSEXUAL HISTORY: SETTINGS, SEQUENCE, AND OUTCOMES

Some mental health professionals prefer the patient's history to emerge from the sessions, as the patient chooses to talk about this and that, guided and reinforced by the therapist's selective "Can you say more about . . . ?" Our preference at the Johns Hopkins Sexual Behaviors Consultation Unit is to obtain a semistructured psychosexual history from patients once they have explained and elaborated on the reasons they are seeking professional help. The history thus obtained is probably incomplete and significant events may be omitted, but an initial semistructured interview does provide the basic skeletal structure of the patient's life story. Coupled with the therapeutic alliance, the history is the foundation of therapy in the life story perspective. The initial history provides the narrative that the therapy amplifies as these and other, initially omitted, life events are recounted and processed for affect and meaning.

The sexual components of the history are obviously significant for the individual with a sexual disorder or dysfunction. Table 6.2 provides a sample of the components that the clinician might gather in a comprehensive psychosexual history. Each component is accompanied by a brief note about why that item might be significant, depending, of course, on the type of narrative being discovered or constructed.

MEANINGFUL CONNECTIONS: UNDERSTANDING VERSUS EXPLANATION

If one distinction holds the key to a successful use of the life story perspective, it is the distinction between *understanding* and *explanation,* as these constructs of the German historian Wilhelm Dilthey were elaborated by Karl Jaspers in his *General Psychopathology* in 1913.(1) The distinctions lies in the type of connectedness attributed to the sequence of life events in the narrative of an individual's life. Is this connectedness a causal link in which a prior event explains (*erklaren*) why a later mental state or life condition exists? Or is does this connectedness entail a reasonably persuasive and powerfully empathic assertion that leads one to understand (*verstehen*) a meaningful connection between a past event and a present mental state or behavior? Hairsplitting? Jaspers was accused of such when he wrote about this distinction. It is not hairsplit-

TABLE 6.2

*Components of a Psychosexual History and Possible Significance of
an Event in the Development of the Individual's Psychosexual Life*

Life Event	Sample Question	Possible Significance for Psychosexual Development
Infancy and Childhood		
Parental holding, feeding, and affection	Do you have any memories of being held as a very young child? When you were hurt and crying, what would you do?	Psychosomatic connectedness with loving other
Childhood illness, injury, or physical disability	Did you have any unusual childhood illnesses, injuries, or hospitalizations?	Relationship with one's body as source of pleasure or pain
First sexual memory	What is your first sexual memory? I'll let you decide what you mean by *sexual*. What were the emotions you felt during this event?	Suggests ways in which the individual thinks about sex and the affect that it bears
Source of sexual knowledge	How did you learn about sex?	Provides more information about parental comfort with sex versus school or street sources
First sexual contact with another	What is the first sexual activity you had with another? Your emotional reaction?	Suggests ways in which the individual thinks about sex and the affect that it bears
Sexual atmosphere in the home	How did your parents handle sexual matters? Would it be a topic of conversation?	Primary cultural environment in which individual absorbs shared meaning of sex
Parents' expression of affection with each other	Did your parents express affection in the presence of others?	Operationalizes the previous question and describes internalized memory of parents
Sibling sexual contact	Did your brother(s)/sister(s) engage in sex play? Please describe it and how long it occurred. Was it forced or painful?	Possible early sexual trauma versus normal age-appropriate play
Nudity, exposure to explicit sexual activity	Were bedrooms shared? Bedroom and bathroom doors closed/locked? Do you recall nudity or	Ruling out hypersexualized (relative to cultural norm) home environment

(continued)

TABLE 6.2 *(continued)*

Life Event	Sample Question	Possible Significance for Psychosexual Development
	explicit sexual media around the house?	
Incest, sexual trauma	As a child, did anyone ever touch you sexually or do anything sexual in your presence that made you feel uncomfortable?	Ruling out sexual trauma; if present, initial reading of emotional aspects

Adolescence

Life Event	Sample Question	Possible Significance for Psychosexual Development
Menarche and development of secondary sexual characteristics	How old were you when you reached puberty? What was your reaction to the changes in your body?	Likely to be the first conscious reaction to mature sexuality
Body image	How did you regard your body and appearance at 13 years of age?	Body self-image at 13 likely to be the core body image of a lifetime
First ejaculation/ masturbation/ orgasm	How old were you when you first masturbated or experienced ejaculation/ orgasm? What were the circumstances and what was your reaction?	Assessment of emotional reaction to sexual pleasure and its integration into self-concept
Primary sexual fantasy	What was the most erotic/ arousing thought or stimulus to you as an adolescent?	As with body image, primary sexual fantasy of adolescence likely to persist as core erotogenic stimulus
Same-sex fantasies and behaviors	Did you have any sexual or romantic experiences with boys/girls? Please describe them and your reaction.	Assessment of emotional reaction to homoerotic attractions and activities and their integration into self-concept
Dating experiences	Please describe your dating experiences, including what type of sexual activity occurred.	Compare patterns of patient to those of his/her peers
First intercourse / genital sex with another	Please describe your first experience of intercourse / genital sex (including your age and age of partner) and your reaction to it.	Assessment of emotional reaction to interpersonal sexual activities and their integration into self-concept
Paraphilic,	(Review the more common	Adolescence typically the

(continued)

TABLE 6.2 (*continued*)

Life Event	Sample Question	Possible Significance for Psychosexual Development
compulsive, and Internet sexual behaviors	paraphilias, asking if the patient ever engaged in the behavior. Quantify time and nature of sexual sites visited on Internet.)	period during which these behaviors begin to emerge
Young Adulthood		
Number and type of sexual partners	About how many sexual partners have you had? How would you describe the types of relationship you had with them? Their genders and ages?	A face validity description of the sexual behavior pattern; compare with peer group norms
Sexual relationships	How did each relationship begin and develop? What were the reasons for its termination? Who initiated the actual breakup?	Assessment of the potential for interpersonal component in sexual relationships
Marital / domestic partner relationships	(As above in sexual relationships, and ask for a description of the courtship and parental reactions to partner.)	Assessment of the potential for interpersonal component in committed or lengthy sexual relationships; further comment on parental attitudes and relationship with patient
Sexual dysfunction	Did you ever have any difficulty functioning sexually?	If positive response, obtain fuller description of conditions that may have been present at beginning and those that may have maintained the dysfunction
Sexually transmitted diseases (STDs)	Have you ever had a sexually transmitted disease? Do you know your HIV status?	May provide information useful in making a medical referral at conclusion of evaluation
Middle Adulthood		
Primary sexual relationship	(Obtain a detailed history of its origins and development, including	A face validity description of the sexual behavior pattern with primary

(*continued*)

TABLE 6.2 *(continued)*

Life Event	Sample Question	Possible Significance for Psychosexual Development
	nonsexual problems: financial, extrarelational partners, drug or alcohol abuse.)	sexual partner; assessment of ability to manage partnership and its vicissitudes
Children	How are the children doing? How do you and your partner manage their discipline?	Opportunity to further assess the quality of empathy with those who should be emotionally close
Infertility/ contraception	Have you had any problems with fertility? Do you practice contraception? What type?	Infertility treatment or pressures possibly associated with sexual dysfunction or ambivalence about child-bearing
Sexual behaviors	How frequently do you have sex? Please describe the typical activities (scripts) you engage in. Any sexual dysfunction?	A face validity description of the sexual behavior pattern with primary sexual partner
Other sexual partners	Have you been sexually active outside your primary relationship? (Assess STD risk with patient.)	A face validity description of the sexual behavior pattern with other sexual partners; assessment of ego-syntonic or ego-dystonic reaction to these extrarelational activities
Presenting sexual problem	(Obtain a detailed history of its development and, for couple, perceived and actual reaction of partner to the problem.)	A face validity description of the sexual behavior pattern; assessment of congruence of perception of problem and attribution of causes by partners
Older Adulthood		
Disease, injury, surgery	(Obtain a detailed chronology of the condition, especially as it relates to presenting sexual problem.)	Assessment of possible role of somatic factors in sexual problem
Attitudes toward limits imposed by	What are your plans for the future? Do you foresee	Assessment of reality testing or denial about

(continued)

TABLE 6.2 *(continued)*

Life Event	Sample Question	Possible Significance for Psychosexual Development
aging and death	any limitations on what you would like to do? What is that like for you? Do you ever use the word *death* when discussing or thinking about the future?	the future; pathological narcissism may use defense of denial
Presenting sexual problem	(Obtain a detailed history of its development and, for couple, perceived and actual reaction of partner to the problem.)	A face validity description of the sexual behavior pattern; assessment of congruence of perception of problem and attribution of causes by partners

ting; it is an important methodological approach to the life narrative that, if not made, perpetuates much of the confusion and dissention among mental health providers today, nearly a century after Jaspers wrote.

Jaspers describes *understanding of meaningful connections* in psychology in this way:

Psychic events "emerge" out of each other in a way that we understand. Attacked people become angry and spring to the defence, cheated persons become suspicious. The way in which such an emergence takes place is understood by us, our understanding is genetic. Thus we understand psychic reactions to experience, we understand the development of passion, the growth of an error, the content of delusion and dream; we understand the effects of suggestion, an abnormal personality in its own context or the inner necessities of someone's life. Finally, we understand how the patient sees himself and how this mode of self-understanding becomes a factor in his psychic development.(1, pp. 302–303)

Jaspers warns, however, of the limitations of understanding meaningful connections:

In any given case the judgment of whether a meaningful connection is real does not rest on its self-evident character alone. It depends primarily on the tangible facts (that is, on the verbal contents, cultural factors, people's acts, ways of life, and expressive gestures) in terms of which the connection is understood, and which provide objective data. All such objective data, however, are always incomplete, and our understanding of any particular, real event has to remain more or less an interpretation with only in a few cases any relatively high degree of complete and convincing objectivity. We understand only so far as such understanding is suggested to us by the objective data of the individual case, that is, by the patients' expressive movements, acts, speech and self-description, etc.(p. 303)

Life stories, psychological narratives, and personal myths are all constructed with the mortar of meaningful connections understood by the patient and the therapist. The meaningful connections are numerous and typically relate to a time span measured in years and decades. The understanding should provide stability and direction; but it should also be recognized for what it is: one of perhaps several possible understandings of the connections in an individual's life.

In therapy, then, the patient and the therapist should hold the meaningful connections suggested by the therapist or discovered by the patient as hypotheses. Only after the meaningful connection is tested through the emotional and rational processing of the hypothesis should it be awarded the position of accepted understanding of past events as they relate to present psychological functioning, And even this understanding should be regarded not as a certainty but as the "best bet" given the objective data available for examination in therapy.

■ Regina, single and 29 years old, was in therapy because of a pattern of casual sexual encounters that she knew was harmful to her. Because of the pattern, she was at risk for contracting a sexually transmitted disease, and she was unable to develop a lasting relationship with a man. She said she wanted marriage and children; but it was clear to her that her behaviors were saying the opposite.

In the initial psychosexual history taking, Regina acknowledged that she had been sexually abused by her stepfather between the ages of 11 and 14. The abuse stopped when the stepfather and her mother divorced. Regina told the therapist that the abuse included sexual intercourse and she was so ashamed that she never told her mother or anyone else about it.

Her teen years were marked by several sexual relationships with young men. Most were brief affairs that consisted of immediate idealization of the relationship, sexual intercourse, and then the breakup initiated by her partner. After a while, Regina no longer romantically idealized the young men, and the sexual encounters became more depersonalized and casual. She had had two abortions and now had herpes.

In the course of the therapy, Regina was able to revisit the years during which she was sexually abused by her stepfather. She recognized not only the pain caused by the violation but also the loss she felt when the stepfather left her mother and herself. About this latter emotion, Regina was most ashamed. The anger she could readily admit; the sense of betrayal and loss was much more difficult to look at in therapy.

As time passed, however, she was able to see that she had idealized her stepfather before the abuse. He was the father she had never had. The abuse was frightening at first, but after a while she was able to distance herself from the experience, saying to herself that it was not really happening. When the stepfather abruptly left the home, Regina was both relieved and grieved. Neither emotion could be shared with her mother.

At about six months into the course of therapy, Regina came to the conclusion that she had transferred to her boyfriends, then her casual partners, the same dynamic she had had with her stepfather: idealization followed by protective distancing and depersonalization. She had formed a meaningful connection in the narrative of her sexual life. With this connection, Regina was able to understand her present behavior in the light of her past experiences. The task of therapy then turned to constructing with her the basis of a new narrative of what she as a woman could be with a man as a potential life partner.

Both Regina and her therapist understood that her sexual relationships with men were probably the result of her experience of being sexually abused by her stepfather. Does this *explain* the phenomenon in the sense of providing certainty about the causal link between abuse and the series of casual sex partners? No, it does not provide certain causality as defined in the physical sciences. Rather, it provides a meaningful connectedness that allows the narrative of Regina's life story to be constructed in a way that provides both understanding of the past and direction to the future.

VARIETIES OF NARRATIVE

We see, therefore, that the life story perspective can depend on theoretical systems that address meaningful connections between past life events (perhaps only perceived) and present sexual problems. Three theorists who have applied their heuristic structures to sexual behaviors are David Scharff, Robert Stoller, and Kurt Freund. Certainly these three do not exhaust extant theories about sexual development, and each would admit an indebtedness to theorists who preceded them. I select their work here to provide descriptions of the sexual narrative structures that are typically encountered by those employed in the understanding of sexual problems and disorders.

Scharff on Reciprocal Psychosomatic Partnership

David Scharff has written on sexual development largely from object relations theory. In *The Sexual Relationship,* (2) Scharff begins with the earliest of life experiences, that of the child relating to mother (or "mothering" parent). He describes how, in a developmental fashion, each stage builds on the achievements of earlier stages, as the individual expresses and finds, or at least searches for, meaning in sexual experiences. He distinguishes object relations theory from more traditional Freudian drive theory: "[Object relations] theory holds that the individual's personality development is determined by the need for and availability of relationships to primary figures in early life, rather than by aggressive or sexual drives seeking an outlet." (p. 2) It is the inner representations of the objects (persons whom the individual relates to) and the response to these objects — not merely the conflict between libidinal drive and the strictures of superego, as a more traditional analytic formulation may present it — that influence subsequent relationships.

For Scharff, foundational to the object relations sexual theory is the construct of *reciprocal psychosomatic partnership*. The initial psychosomatic partnership is between child and mothering parent. Later, the reciprocal psychosomatic partnership is reenacted and responded to in adult sexual relationships in which the bodies of two persons are vehicles for a psychosomatic partnership. Scharff describes it thus:

> The infant relates to his mother through using his body and hers. She relates similarly to him, and within this physical context their mutual feelings of attachment, concern, and pleasure grow. In this process, the nursing couple develops a reciprocal psychosomatic partnership. The neurological capacities of the infant mature in the context of this support from mother and family which is required if he is to learn the uses of his body, interpret his bodily feelings and to understand the meaning of his body in experience with the environment.

. . . Adult couples need a similar psychosomatic partnership to interpret their own sexual urges and functioning — the psychological signals and potential that mean nothing until given an interpersonal environment. They need each other to fulfill individual potential. In the interaction of meeting the physical needs, a bridge is formed not only between their two object worlds, but also between the soma and psyche inside each of them. The bridge provides each person new opportunities to rework old issues that, for many people, are rekindled most vividly within their sexual life. The sexual life of the parents is a source for strengthening bonds within themselves and the larger family, but it is also an area that will reflect any difficulty in those wider family bonds. (pp. 4–5)

Scharff's construct of reciprocal psychosomatic partnership can serve to make meaningful connections between events of childhood or early life and later sexual problems. A child having a severe case of eczema may be impeded from experiencing her body as a source of loving connectedness to her parents. The pain and itch are far too distracting to sense the tendering and love behind the parental embrace. The body is not a vehicle for comfort and pleasure as much as it is a tormentor that alienates her from others. When this woman later in life reports hypoactive sexual desire, it is possible that the internalized relational experiences of childhood related to her eczema may provide some meaningful point of developmental departure. The task of the therapy will be to test the developmental connections of this childhood experience with the present low desire for her partner. One certainly cannot simply assert the connection as causal fact. Other childhood experiences of body, the heightened attention on body during adolescence, and, of course, earlier sexual experiences will need to be explored to see whether, in fact, there has been a pattern in which her body does not serve her as a means to achieving a reciprocal, caring, psychosomatic partnership.

Stoller on Transvestitic Fetishism

Among his many writings about gender and sexual development, Robert Stoller applies psychoanalytic theory to individuals with transvestitic cross-dressing behavior. In his *Presentations of Gender,* (3) Stoller describes the heterosexual male who cross-dresses for sexual arousal and masturbatory release as one who, in this behavior, is reenacting a childhood trauma in which he perceived himself as being degraded — usually by a woman. The result of the early childhood trauma was a narcissistically wounded young boy who would carry with him into adulthood an impaired sense of his own masculinity. Stoller writes, "One frequently finds that in early childhood the boy was cross-dressed by a girl or a woman for the purpose of humiliating him. In time, the humiliation is converted, via the perversion (of fetishistic cross-dressing) to a triumph, especially as manifested by the ability to achieve an erection and orgasm despite being in women's clothes."(p. 22) In his summary discussion of a particular case, Stoller elaborates on the developmental factors that he saw as contributory to adult transvestitic cross-dressing:

> A little boy who has already developed a male core identity — a conviction, an acceptance, a body of knowledge that he is a male — nonetheless has a developing masculinity more vulnerable to threat than other boys'. With Tim, the factors that weakened gender identity development were the cleft palate, which disappointed his mother and made her identify with him (and thereby build the sense of flawedness into him); inadequate mouth structure for normal feeding as an infant; the minor speech defect, which marked him as different in early childhood; the surgery to repair his palate; her not being with him for the ten days following surgery; the severe febrile illness that — perhaps producing minimal brain damage — left his personality permanently changed from enthusiasm to sadness and with a dull normal intelligence; his mother's continuous, usually covert anger and disappointment in him; his parents' gradually deteriorating marriage; his father's being passive and distant when he was around and often not present; the disruption by constant moves; the birth of a sibling, a girl who was desired and who made mother happy.
>
> If a boy with a compromised sense of intactness and worth is then cross-dressed — especially for two years by a girl with powerful transsexual impulses — he is, I suspect, at high risk for transvestism.(p. 151)

In his formulation of the case, Stoller enumerates the multiple occurrences in Tim's infancy and childhood that put him "at high risk" for transvestism. Stoller's restraint is admirable here in that he does not assert a causal relationship between the past events, the presumed psychological trauma, and the resulting adult transvestism. Instead, he offers a cogent understanding of meaningful connections that may have resulted in Tim's present psychological status and his cross-dressing behaviors. In remarking that the febrile illness in childhood may have caused minimal brain damage and accompanying personality alterations in Tim, Stoller is also suggesting that one should consider factors from the disease perspective.

Freund on Courtship Disorders

Both Scharff and Stoller drew from the analytic tradition as they applied theory to understanding sexual behavior. Kurt Freund drew on the terminology of animal behaviorists, who refer to precopulatory procreative behaviors as *courtship behavior*, as he described the behaviors of voyeurism, exhibitionism, telephone scatologia, frotteurism, and preferential rape as disorders of the "courtship process."(4) In doing so, Freund brought the anthropomorphism of the animal behaviorists full circle.

Freund describes the normal courtship process in males of many species as one that involves (i) a *finding phase,* in which the potential partner is perceived; (ii) an *affiliative phase,* in which the partner is engaged in some activity; (iii) a *tactile phase,* in which touching occurs; and (iv) a *copulatory phase,* in which intercourse occurs. According to this paradigm, voyeurism is a disruption in the finding phase; exhibitionism and telephone scatologia, disorders of the affiliative phase; frotteurism, a disruption of the tactile phase; and some forms of preferential rape, disorders of the copulatory phase. Sadism and masochism could be a disorder of either the affiliative or the touching phase, depending on the nature of the sadistic or masochistic behavior — that is, whether with or without tactile contact.

Freund's hypothesis of courtship disorder is an interesting construct and, to give him due credit, he tested its validity with designed research.(5,6) The construct of *courtship* enables us to conceptualize and group many of the paraphilic behaviors in a seemingly meaningful order. What it does not do, of course, is clarify why an individual has the syndrome of courtship disorder behaviors. Putative etiologies such as hypersexuality, fear of intimate and consenting intercourse, or dysfunctional social learning about sexual relationship (e.g., in a person with a childhood and adolescence of attention deficit disorder) are all unproven but eminently testable, as Freund would have urged.

The life story perspective may employ the courtship disorder construct, especially if the focus of the therapy is on the peripubertal phase of the patient's life. In exploring the genesis of adult paraphilic behaviors, there may be meaningful connections with this period that can provide an understanding of why courtship behaviors did not develop normally. Social learning theory would then provide the ground for developing strategies to remediate the normal behaviors and compensate for adult deficiencies in the courtship-disorder paraphilia.

ESSENTIALISM VERSUS SOCIAL CONSTRUCTIONISM

No discussion of meaningful connections should be had without acknowledging again (see Chapter 5) the extensive discussion and often heated debate between two camps of theorists usually labeled *essentialists* and *social constructionists*. Essentialists are in the Aristotelian tradition and assert that true "essences" in external realities can be known and named as such. A dog is a dog because of its essence, "dogness." Furthermore, that dogness can be known by us and its bearer labeled *dog*. Social constructionism in the social sciences developed from the anthropological and sociological work of Margaret Mead and Talcott Parsons. The basic and fundamental assertion of social constructionism is that "reality is socially constructed" by the language.(7) Through the use of language, cultures and subgroups within cultures bring meanings to the chaos of the inherently meaningless reality of the external world. For social constructionists, there is no "dogness" out there in the external world. There is the agreed-upon construct that *dog* is different from the construct *wolf* or *coyote*. All constructs are different because social groups have made them such.

This doggedly simplistic paragraph certainly does not do justice to the complexity of the debate between essentialism and social constructionism. But it may serve to alert the reader to the huge theoretical differences among those who engage in the discussion of "meaning" in human life. These differences do not become less in the discussion of meaning of sexual behavior. Indeed, some have concluded that, when applied to human sexuality, these two systems — essentialism and social constructionism — cannot be conjoined.(8)

On the essentialist side of the debate in sexuality are those who are guided by the reality of the biological body — its genetic structure, its hormones, its circadian rhythms, and its state of disease or health. They assert that there is a natural function that flows from this biological basis, a function that is "out there" whether or not we acknowledge it or make it such by our language. On a popular level, the parents of a baby boy who strive to avoid gender stereotyping express this essentialism when, having previously raised his sister through infancy, they reluctantly admit, "There is a difference between boys and girls." The force of biology on gender and sexual definition is poignantly described in *As Nature Made Him*, a biography of a young man who as a child suffered a penectomy, was raised as a girl, and then as a young "woman" decided to live as a male again.(9) Essentialists find support in such anecdotal reports and view sexual behaviors of males and females as in part determined by the somatic reality of their different bodies.(10) They hold that with this basis in biology, sexual behavior can be predicted; it can be judged as statistically normal or abnormal.

Social constructionists in the field of human sexuality, led by the seminal work of John Gagnon and William Simon, say, in Gagnon's words, "Sexuality is not . . . [a] universal phenomenon which is the same in all historical times and cultural spaces."(11, p. 3) It is rather an expression of sexual scripts developed and given meaning by culture. These scripts are the result of a variety of social factors within the culture and serve a variety of social functions. There is no "one way" for sexual behaviors that is applicable to all peoples. For social constructionists, sexual "variations" are the focus of attention. Universal norms are nonexistent. The meaning of a sexual behavior is relative to the social context in which it occurs and to the scripts expressed in the behavior. If there are differences between boys and girls, it is because of the cultural factors that have stereotyped the gender roles. Even the body itself is gender specific because of the social meanings that the culture has given to it.(12)

The perspectives methodology does not resolve the conflict between essentialism and social constructionism. But the four perspectives do provide the means to further understand the contributions of both theoretical positions. The disease perspective, with its categories of diseases and physiological causality, is solidly in the essentialist camp. Similarly, the dimension perspective, with its reliance on replication of phenomena and standardized measurement, is also weighed on the essentialist side of the debate. However, the other two perspectives, behavior and life story, are quite compatible with a social constructionist hermeneutic of the sexual phenomena under discussion. Thus essentialism and social constructionism may be disjunctive in their pure theoretical positions, but they can be used conjunctively within a perspectives methodology. What is required of the clinician is the ability to hold and use conflicting approaches at the same time by means of an eclecticism that is both art and science.

DYADIC THERAPY: THE ONE AND THE MANY REVISITED

One of the major philosophical disputes throughout the ages has been the problem of "the one and the many." Whether the dispute employs the terminology of quantum physics or of theology, the question is, does reality consist of one unified element or is it composed of many elements interacting in an orderly manner or in random chaos? Expressions of "the one and the many" debate are seen in polarities such as monotheism versus polytheism; rights of the individual versus rights of the greater community; narcissistic needs versus altruistic responsibilities. Given that the expressions take many forms, it is no surprise to see that this dispute also has correlates in human sexuality. Posed most simply, the question might be, are sex and sexual behaviors basically individual rights or are they basically relational or communitarian in nature?

For the social constructionist, the response is that sex and sexual behaviors are either individual or relational, depending on the social context in which they exist and are considered. The task is to further describe the context so that the shades of individual rights versus relational responsibility can be further discussed. Note that the operative words are *described* and *discussed;* these are the tools of social constructionism, as opposed to *defined* and *decided,* terms much more compatible with an essentialist position.

For the essentialist, then, the question of the individual versus relational quality of sexual behavior takes on a more definitive quality. Human sexuality is seen in a teleological context. There is a goal, a purpose that evolutionary nature or God has "designed" in human sexual behavior. Reproduction, intimacy, and pleasure are the most commonly accepted goals of a sexual teleology. Mature consent between partners is a goal, if not an intrinsic condition. The essentialists admit that sexual acts can certainly occur without any of these goals being sought and without consent being obtained; but sex in its "fullest" expression is open to all the goals possible between consenting partners. For those of essentialist leanings, all human sexuality is fundamentally a relational reality. Even in solitary masturbation, there is usually a "relationship" with an imagined object, even if in its most narcissistic expression it is a relationship of self-pleasuring or anxiety reduction with one's own body. Sexual development over the lifespan is the achievement of interpersonal skills that make possible the expression of intimacy, mutual pleasuring, and, at least in the psychological sense, generativity.

This "one and many" question plays a subtle role in the life story perspective. It is a role that draws on both the essentialist and the social constructionist positions. If sexuality is relational, as I believe it is, then the sexual narrative is likewise relational, not only in content but also in construction. In dyadic sexual therapy there is a collaboration in the reconstruction of a common narrative. There are multiple stories: each partner's individual story and, from their meeting onward, their shared story. Dyadic sexual therapy respects the need for two individual narratives to be told and meaningful connections made. In addition to respecting the integrity of each partner's story and that each story will continue, the work of dyadic therapy is to assist the couple to construct a shared narrative that gives direction and enthusiasm to their future.

ETHICAL CONSIDERATIONS

For the clinician who seeks to employ the life story perspective in therapy, there are two main ethical considerations: (i) be intellectually grounded in at least one theoretical system; but (ii) do not, through selection bias or contrived causation (as described above), *impose* the heuristic structure of this theoretical system on the events or emotional reactions that the patient is describing. Both of these "ethical" considerations are, of course, consistent with proper clinical treatment and should not be seen as new demands. Viktor Frankl, in describing his method of logotherapy, spoke of the collaboration of patient and therapist in putting the logos on the mythos, putting the words to the story.(13) Described this way, the ethical work of the therapist is to help patients verbalize the conscious and preconscious events into a logical narrative that gives direction and meaning to their life.

SUMMARY

The life story perspective is the perspective that discovers and gives further direction to the narrative of an individual's life. The happenings, events, and encounters of the individual's life are placed in a context and sequence from which patient and therapist make meaningful connections. The narrative may be consistent with any of the developmental theories that are respected today. What is crucial is that the narrative respects the actual events that occurred and the meanings attributed to these events by the values of the individual. Developing a life narrative and finding meaning is a collaborative work between patient and therapist in therapy; narrative and meaning are not constructs imposed by the therapist. The life narrative includes the sexual dimension, because sex is an intrinsic part of the human story. More than the other three perspectives, the life story perspective provides an appreciation of the uniqueness of the individual who is seeking professional assistance as a patient. Because of this, all treatment modalities should be informed by the life story perspective.

■ 7

INTEGRATING
THE PERSPECTIVES

 To work successfully with the perspectives, the therapist needs to select the primary perspective that best fits the patient and then integrate the other perspectives into the formulation and treatment to make use of the additional contributions they may provide. Each of the other three perspectives will have some salience for a case. How much each will contribute depends on the clinical characteristics of the case.

The *primary perspective* is determined by the circumstances of the case as elaborated by the complete psychological history, history of the present disorder, and mental status examination. For example, a hypersexual state that is clearly correlated with a bipolar manic episode requires the disease perspective as the primary perspective. Or, to take another example, repeated use of the Internet for sexual arousal at work by an otherwise psychiatrically healthy man would most likely require the behavior perspective as the primary perspective.

The *secondary perspectives* are the remaining three perspectives as they are employed and integrated into the formulation and treatment plan. There is no set hierarchy or order in integrating the other three perspectives. Each must be reviewed and allotted its proper weight or salience, depending on what it can contribute to the formulation and treatment plan. The adequacy of the review of the remaining three perspectives depends on clinicians' competency in each of the perspectives and on their ability to shift from one perspective to another. As mentioned in Chapter 1, few clinicians have equal competency in all four perspectives. Every clinician should be competent in one perspective. Many have a command of two perspectives, and some have a command of three. But only the rare master clinician is totally competent in all four perspectives. For this reason, working successfully with the perspectives typically involves working successfully with colleagues who can complement the formulation of a case with their particular competencies. The perspectives methodology requires clinicians not only to shift their own cognitive sets but also to establish effective collaborations with colleagues who have different areas of expertise.

Using this distinction between primary and secondary perspectives, this chapter describes how the other three perspectives typically are integrated with a primary perspective in the formulation and treatment of a sexual disorder. I consider each of the four perspectives in turn as a primary perspective, and then issues relating to the integration of the remaining three perspectives, labeled as secondary. The point is not to establish an order among these added perspectives but to acknowledge that each is secondary to and integrated within the primary perspective.

THE DISEASE PERSPECTIVE AS PRIMARY TREATMENT PERSPECTIVE

The hallmark of treatment in the disease perspective is the somatic treatment of the patient in order to cure or affect the expression of the sexual disorder or dysfunction. Common examples are sildenafil (Viagra) for erectile dysfunction, vaginal lubricants for dyspareunia, and antiandrogens for hypersexual or predatory sexual behaviors. Also involved in the use of the disease perspective as the primary treatment perspective is the medical treatment of illnesses and conditions that cause sexual disorders and dysfunctions. Examples here are antidepressants for major depression that may cause sexual dysfunction, mood stabilizers for bipolar disorders that cause hypersexual behaviors, and antispasm medication for neurological diseases that may be exacerbated during sexual excitement. The primary goal of the disease perspective is to remedy the bodily part or function that is compromised by disease or physiological dysfunction. Because of the often absorbing nature of the disease or the somatic intervention, working with the disease perspective as the primary treatment perspective tends to dominate the attention of patient and clinician alike. The challenge is to give due consideration to the integration of the other perspectives in the individual's treatment plan.

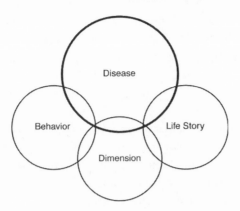

Disease Perspective Primary, Life Story Perspective Secondary

The life story perspective is a likely secondary treatment perspective when the illness or condition (e.g., postsurgical status) has challenged the patient's view of his or her life — its meaning and mortality. A couple that has just been through a prostatectomy as a treatment for cancer may have a sexual dysfunction rooted in both the physical and psychological effects of the surgery. Somatic intervention such as Viagra may be helpful in restoring erectile functioning. But to ignore the life story issues of the meaning of the cancer, the meaning of sexual expression, and the reminder of mortality that the cancer has brought is to miss the important integration of the life story perspective into the primary somatic treatment of the sexual dysfunction.

If the life story treatment is not integrated into the disease perspective treatment when there is ample indication that it should be, the result will seem to be "tossing a pill" at a condition without giving due regard to the psychological issues. The treatment may be solving a problem, but it will miss the psychological and interpersonal context in which the sexual problem has arisen. In such a situation, the couple that has just faced prostate cancer will have an erection available to them with Viagra, but they will not have been helped to address the questions of life and death that the prostate cancer has raised. Similarly, the ejaculatory latency of a man with premature ejaculation may be increased with use of an SSRI, but the treatment will not affect his exaggerated fear of not pleasing his partner. The use of the life story perspective as a secondary treatment intervention can address these issues of meaning and meaningful connections.

Disease Perspective Primary, Behavior Perspective Secondary

The behavior perspective is secondary to the disease perspective for cases in which a sexual behavior pattern is related to the disease process or condition. Perhaps the most common instance is the situation in which somatic treatment has begun for a couple with sexual dysfunction. A penile prosthesis or Viagra has been the primary treatment intervention, but even with erectile capacity optimized, the partners are not engaging with each other sexually. A behavioral intervention of sensate focus therapy is then begun as the secondary treatment perspective.

Another example of the behavior perspective as secondary to the disease perspective is the case in which the sexual behavior is directly related to the state of the disease. Comorbid paraphilic disorders are more likely to be acted out during an episode of affective illness. Two behaviors become the object of treatment intervention: medication compliance for the affective illness and avoidance of the trigger situations that prompt the sexual behavior. The secondary behavior perspective prompts the clinician and patient to develop strategies to reinforce taking the prescribed medications and avoiding the triggers.

It is difficult to imagine how integration of the behavior perspective into a primary disease perspective intervention might pose a negative risk for the overall treatment of a patient. It general, the behavior perspective challenges the patient to take behavioral responsibility for the effects or the sustaining causes of the disease state. This provides a reminder that it is not only what the patient has that is important for treatment but also what the patient does.

Disease Perspective Primary, Dimension Perspective Secondary

A major disease is usually a severe stressor for the individual and his or her partner. Both are forced to deal with limits of energy, mobility, and interest, and, in some foreshadowing, with the ultimate limit of death. For a person with major disease, personality strengths and vulnerabilities can, in many ways, make this time the best of seasons and the worst of seasons. In terms of sexual life, major disease may remove what was once spontaneous and taken for granted and replace it with an interaction that is a reminder of limitations of function and desire. What was simple has now become horribly complex.

When employed secondary to the disease perspective, the dimension perspective is mindful of the individual's personality strengths and weaknesses as he or she encounters the limitations imposed by the illness or postsurgical condition. The woman who has had a double mastectomy and who has a sturdy sense of self is likely to respond to the trauma better than does a husband who, with his low assertiveness and low openness to feelings, is likely to endure the somatic trauma without mutually sharing the emotional aftershock. The clinician who has knowledge of these personality traits will be able to employ them successfully when the couple begins therapy to reestablish their sexual intimacy.

The use of any somatic treatment for sexual dysfunction may be a narcissistic injury for a couple. The sexual arousal facilitated by medication, injection, topical application, vacuum pump, or prosthesis is not a completely natural outcome of sexual attraction and stimulation. It is an assisted response. The "crutch" of the somatic treatment is both necessary and an "insult" to personal abilities. As with the more serious limits of major illness, the limits of somatically assisted sexual response impose a stressor on the couple. For clinician and patients, the dimension perspective places this stressor in the context of personality strengths and vulnerabilities. As the secondary treatment perspective, it invites the treatment plan to use partners' personality strengths and minimize reliance on those traits that are likely to respond feebly to the changed manner of sexual expression.

As when the life story and behavior perspectives are secondary to the disease perspective intervention, it is highly unlikely that use of the dimension perspective as secondary will have any result other than enriching the treatment plan. The natural dominance of the disease perspective is well served when any of the other treatment perspectives are appropriately applied to complement the medical therapy. Each of the other three perspectives serves to refocus the attention and efforts of the patient and clinician on the individual or couple with the sexual problem. Each states that the matter is more than the disease; the person's or couple's sexual life is affected by the disease.

THE BEHAVIOR PERSPECTIVE AS PRIMARY TREATMENT PERSPECTIVE

When the behavior perspective is the primary perspective in formulating a case and developing a treatment plan, the focus is on stopping unwanted sexual behaviors (as in sexual offenses) or starting wanted sexual behaviors (as in sexual dysfunctions).

Behavior Perspective Primary, Disease Perspective Secondary

The most common expression of the disease perspective as secondary to behavior perspective is a pharmacological augmentation of the behavioral treatment. In a couple's sensate focus therapy for erectile disorder, a somatic treatment (oral medication, injections) is added. In a group therapy for men with unwanted sexual behavior, a group member who

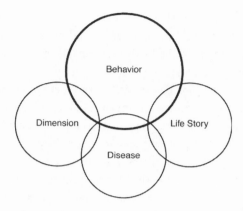

seems unable to stop the behavior through his own efforts takes an SSRI or an antiandrogen. These are two examples of the disease perspective as secondary: an adjunctive somatic treatment is used while the behavioral treatment remains the primary focus.

The clinical challenge in the integration of the somatic treatment is to continue to pay attention to the goals of the behavioral treatment and not to rely on the power of the drug to solve the problem. In sensate focus therapy, the couple must continue to explore how they can establish a relaxed, nondemanding, and sensual rapport with each other when they are attempting to be sexual. In group therapy, the member taking the medication must continue to learn about the triggers of his unwanted sexual behaviors and how to avoid them. Patients' taking personal responsibility for their behavioral program must be seen as primary.

Behavior Perspective Primary, Dimension Perspective Secondary
The dimension perspective is secondary to the behavior perspective when the behaviors that are the object of treatment are expressions of or closely related to personality traits or cognitive vulnerabilities. If, for example, the sexual dysfunction is associated with avoidant personality traits, or the use of prostitutes is connected with excitement-seeking traits, then it is likely that the personality traits will also be the object of the treatment interventions. Cognitive-behavioral therapy is a particularly appropriate treatment modality when dimensional traits are closely allied with behavioral problems.

The dimension perspective also assists the work of the behavioral therapy by striving to identify those environmental and psychological stressors that, because of an individual's particular vulnerabilities, act as triggers. Thus, attention is given not only to triggers that are more proximate and behavioral (e.g., surfing the Internet for sexually explicit sites for masturbation) but also to more subtle, more temporally remote or "upstream" triggers that lead to the unwanted sexual behavior (e.g., lack of assertiveness with partner).

The clinical challenge for integrating the dimension perspective with the primary behavior perspective in the treatment plan is the possible "drift" from behaviors to attitudes as the focus of therapy. This is an especially likely collusion between patient and therapist when the behaviors in question are sexual. There is a natural tendency, rooted in an understandable reticence, to avoid talking explicitly about personal sexual behaviors. Thus the "issues" processed in the therapy may drift from what happens sexually to questions of personal attitudes or marital dynamics. Unfortunately, this may result in an avoidance of addressing the sexual behaviors themselves and the sexual behavioral interventions that are intended to be primary.

Behavior Perspective Primary, Life Story Perspective Secondary

The life story perspective is typically secondary to the behavior perspective at two moments in the course of treatment. The first is when the patient is in the initial phase of treatment and wants to have some understanding of how this sexual disorder entered his or her life. This is usually done with broad descriptive strokes, with minimal challenge or interpretation suggested by the therapist. During this initial phase, the patient has a working hypothesis of meaningful connections concerning the genesis of the behavior. Given this initial working hypothesis, the therapy then usually reverts to the primary work of stopping or starting the behavior in question.

The second point when the life story perspective emerges usually occurs after the behavior has been controlled. When the behavioral treatment has been effective in stopping an unwanted behavior, the patient has experienced a loss. There is a vacancy in the individual's needs that the unwanted behavior had attempted to fill. An alcoholic person speaks of the loss of a friend (in the bottle) and perhaps loss of a social environment in which the drinking occurred. There are obvious parallels in sexual behaviors. Depression and demoralization may ensue, and these should be addressed to reduce the risk of relapse. At this point in therapy, especially with patients who have sufficient cognitive skills and psychological curiosity about their lives, another phase of life story work should begin. While depression may require somatic interventions, the life story perspective is the principal approach for addressing demoralization. At this point, the examination of the narrative is more detailed and challenging than at the beginning of therapy. In addition to the external stressors that may have played a role in the emergence of the behavioral problem, the intrapsychic conflicts are more accessible now and can be addressed in terms of the role they may have played in initiating or maintaining the behavior.

In both treatment phases, the life story perspective works with the meanings that the individual attributes to the sexual behaviors that are the focus of treatment. In some cases, the work will involve a reconstruction of new meaning. This may be seen in the case of the individual who has used sexual partners solely for personal gratification or for control. Finding intimacy and mutual gratification as a component of sexual expression may alter the meaning attributed to sexual intercourse. For other individuals, the meanings once attributed to sexual interaction (e.g., self-worth, proof of attractiveness) may have to be found in other, nonsexual behaviors and interactions. These individuals will need to find self-esteem in activities that are not limited to sexual encounters.

The clinical challenge of integrating the life story perspective into the behavior perspective treatment is similar to that of integrating the dimension perspective: the possibility of collusion between therapist and patient to avoid the behavioral work that must be done. Insight alone is hardly ever sufficient to stop a sexual disorder or to remedy a sexual dysfunction. The factors that led to a behavior are usually not those that sustain its expression. The behavior perspective focuses on the behavior in the here and now, identifying the factors that are helpful and those that stand in the way of treatment goals. Life story therapy focusing on factors that may have played a role in the origins of the behavior may be a hindrance to the primary work that must now be done: to address the factors allowing or causing the behavior to persist.

THE DIMENSION PERSPECTIVE AS PRIMARY TREATMENT PERSPECTIVE

The dimension perspective is concerned with an individual's constellation of personality traits and cognitive abilities as he or she responds to the demands of the various situations of life. In issues of treatment, the dimension perspective takes measure of these traits and develops strategies — both cognitive and behavioral — that will facilitate a more adaptive response to the stress of the environment. This perspective does not address issues of presumed causality or developmental etiology. The di-

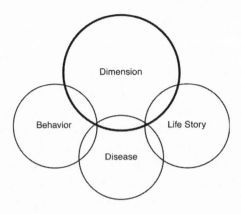

mension perspective is cross-sectional measurement. The other perspectives are needed to give the treatment texture and fullness. Therefore, to the extent that the other three perspectives can complement the cross-sectional view of the individual with information about somatic conditions, behavioral patterns, or meaningful developmental connections, then to that same extent will the primary dimension perspective be enriched and, hopefully, become a more effective treatment.

Dimension Perspective Primary, Life Story Perspective Secondary

The dimension perspective describes individuals' profiles as they are measured, usually by self-reported personality measures. It does not provide any direct information on how these traits happened to develop in a particular individual. The patient reports, "I am anxious in most social situations; I am especially anxious in intimate and sexual situations." In making this report, the patient concretizes and validates the finding of high trait anxiety on the personality inventory. "I guess I have always been that way, especially since that first crash-and-burn relationship in high school when I got dumped." This further comment is an opening to the life story perspective that will provide some understanding—initially presumed to be part of the meaningful connection—of the high social anxiety trait.

Employing the life story perspective as secondary to the dimension perspective can provide historical and developmental support to what otherwise might be dismissed as a state finding on a personality inventory. A patient's statement such as "I was anxious about the evaluation when I answered those questions; I can't be that anxious compared with others in general" is often the devaluation of trait to state in a personality inventory finding. Recalling other times when the trait was expressed, times when it was not, and the individual's various responses to the situations is often very helpful life story therapy work. It both provides examples of presumed developmental incidents and suggests how the trait might be strengthened or made less salient.

The challenge of the secondary use of the life story perspective is to guard against avoiding the present, the here-and-now stress-filled situations or relationship, through a flight to a safer incident in the past. For some, such diversions may be flavored with self-justifying recollections that assume a moral masochist victim role ("I am an innocent victim of what others have done to me"). Employing the life story perspective secondary to the dimension perspective permits appropriate, even frequent, retrospections into past situations. But the therapist will assist the patient to use the recollection by applying it to the here-and-now situation: "You seemed to survive the breakup of that relationship very well. I wonder what the differences were that made that possible for you." This sets the stage for the application of the past experience to the present expression of anxiety in an intimate relationship.

Dimension Perspective Primary, Disease Perspective Secondary

As the life story perspective complements with the meaningful narrative, so the disease perspective complements the primary dimension perspective by providing a possible somatic etiology for the traits that have been measured. This etiology may be the physiologically based temperament or a clearly disease-related condition such as affective illness, multi-infarct dementia, or an autistic syndrome. The dimension perspective is focused on assisting the person to use cognitive and personality resources to respond to the demands of the present life situation. For an individual with significant findings from the disease perspective, the treatment plan should be informed with this knowledge. In the treatment of sexual disorders and dysfunctions, this generally means tailoring the treatment to the limitations imposed by the disease state. Group therapy is often the treatment of choice. It employs an efficient use of resources for disparate conditions as well as the general curative factors of group therapy. Examples of such groups are therapy for post–cancer surgery patients and cognitively impaired sex offenders, and sex education for mentally retarded adolescents and adults.

The main risk factors in employing the disease perspective secondary to the dimension perspective in treating sexual disorders and dysfunctions result from the integration of the two perspectives in group therapy. The first risk is that patients become unduly segregated from mainstream social contact. The second is that the individual differences within the group will not be recognized and addressed with appropriate treatment interventions. Both of these risks can be minimized if group therapists take periodic evaluations and remedial actions.

Dimension Perspective Primary, Behavior Perspective Secondary

The behavior perspective easily serves as secondary to the dimension perspective in the treatment of sexual disorders and dysfunctions. The dimension perspective identifies the situations in which the individual's personality traits or cognitive abilities are overtaxed and his or her responses are disordered or dysfunctional. The behavior perspective provides the treatment modality, often cognitive-behavioral, to remedy the response and adaptation to the situation. In the reciprocal disinhibition of sensate focus therapy, the anxiety of the couple in sexual situations is gradually replaced by relaxation and mutual sensual pleasure. In the design and discussion of the sexual exercises, treatment also addresses issues of assertiveness and dependency. What makes the dimension perspective primary is that the starting point of the treatment interventions is the personality traits and the behaviors that express the traits. This not only is true at the beginning of therapy but is constant throughout the therapy.

In the treatment of sexual offenders or persons with severe personality traits, the interventions often have as a goal the development of empathy. This is a dimension perspective goal. The interventions to reach that goal are likely to be cognitive-behavioral. This, again, is an example of the behavior perspective serving as a complement to the primary dimension perspective.

THE LIFE STORY PERSPECTIVE AS PRIMARY TREATMENT PERSPECTIVE

The meaning of what the patient has encountered in his or her lifetime is the key focus of treatment in the life story perspective. A story has been written, and the narrative has come to a decision point or crisis that requires meaningful attention. The therapist's role is to help the individual make conscious the preconscious assumptions or unconscious conflicts that have been formative. Given the daylight of conscious attention, these assumptions or conflicts can be reinterpreted or reconstructed to give new meanings that facilitate a more vibrant direction to living, working, loving, and, ultimately, facing death.

The other three perspectives are integrated into the life story perspective by assessing the meanings attached to the behavior, the disease, or the trait. Of all the perspectives, primary treatment in the life story perspective should be the easiest in which to integrate the remaining three perspectives. Yet in practice it often proves to be the most difficult.

The problem lies in the power of the narrative. Deep within the roots of human culture, the need to find meaning in the events of personal and group life has always existed. Creation narratives, accounts of the beginnings of the tribe or nation, epic tales of heroes and heroines, and personal stories woven together to tell others how one has arrived at the present — all are powerful components of human intercourse. These narratives are invested with elemental religious, patriotic, and narcissistic values. Reject the cultural narrative and one risks excommunication, rejection by peers, or charges of treason. Lose or reject the personal narrative and one reaches a state of existential crisis. The elemental power of the narrative has a grip on storyteller and listener, therapist and patient, that is often hypnotic. Religious cults, militant nationalism, and a narcissism blind to the needs of others are the manifestations of the power of narratives over groups and individuals. The narrative is not easily modified; it is hardly ever successfully challenged. And yet this is precisely the task of the other three perspectives — to challenge the operative narrative by offering information that requires the individual's meaning attribution function to consider new realities and, perhaps, to construct a new story.

Life Story Perspective Primary, Disease Perspective Secondary

It is the rare depressed person who initially attributes the depression to disregulation of CNS neurotransmitters. The attributions are usually this loss or that tragic event. "Who wouldn't be depressed, after what I've been through" is the common assessment of the new patient. The life story narrative has reached a nadir because of the events that have happened, and the individual is seeking help.

Enter the disease perspective as a secondary perspective. Family history and previous "episodes" strikingly similar to the present levels of sleep, appetite, energy, and sexual interest suggest that perhaps something else is at work here: a disease process. It is usually accepted as such when the patient has responded successfully to an antidepressant medication and can admit to self and others that a "chemical imbalance" had existed. While there are still real losses and tragic events to manage, it was the chemical imbalance that caused the severity of the depression. The losses are demoralizing; the chemical imbalance was depressing.

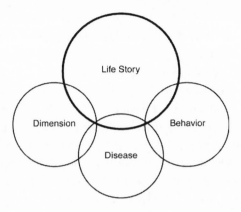

In the sexual arena, integration of the disease perspective into the primary life story perspective should occur when there are somatic contributions to the sexual disorders. The most common examples are hypoactive sexual desire linked to major depression, thyroid disease, and chronic illness. The challenge of the integration is to allot the proper salience to the disease and, at the same time, to continue to process the meaningful connections the patient can make to the sexual disorder. Mental health professionals trained in the nonmedical sciences (psychology, social work) may have to exert special care to "pay attention to the body" as they treat such patients. The power of the narrative may trump the insidious somatic condition, and collusion between therapist and patient in the elaboration of the story may, in fact, result in failure to seek proper medical attention for the problem.

Life Story Perspective Primary, Behavior Perspective Secondary

The most important truth to remember in integrating the behavior perspective into the life story perspective is that the conditions that initially started a behavior may not be those that maintain and reinforce it. In twelve-step meetings, it is a common technique for participants to introduce themselves and then to tell their story — often described by Alcoholics Anonymous members as the drunkalogue. But the collective wisdom of AA does not allow a member to drone on and on about the episodes, sadness, and losses of the past without a sharp refocusing in the present. What is important is whether or not the member is "working the program" daily in the present. While a review of the past may enrich the understanding of the present and instruct others in the course of alcoholism in a fellow member, by itself it is not usually sufficient to stop the drinking or to maintain sobriety. To achieve this, the person must constantly work the behavioral twelve steps. Working the twelve steps in the present counters the conditions that, if unaddressed, would promote a resumption of drinking.

The AA approach to story and behavior is a useful model for integration of the behavior perspective into the life story perspective. While an understanding of the meaningful connections in the beginnings of a sexual disorder is enriching, it is not usually sufficient to provide motivation to stop problematic behaviors or to begin desired behaviors. Accomplishing this requires some of the techniques of the behavior perspective. For those mental health therapists whose life story theory (e.g., psychoanalytic) is averse to employing behavioral techniques (e.g., group therapy that focuses on trigger identification), this may prove an insurmountable challenge. No argument can be made with such a therapist if the sexual behaviors are being controlled or expressed according to treatment goals. But if the sexual behaviors remain problematic while the life story elaboration continues and continues, then a clinical disservice is being done to the patient. In such cases, ongoing treatment should be supplemented by a colleague with behavioral treatment skills, or the patient should be referred to another therapist who can more competently integrate the life story and behavior perspectives.

Life Story Perspective Primary, Dimension Perspective Secondary

The integration of the dimension perspective into the life story perspective usually is transparent and is achievable from the beginning of therapy. The therapist has been informed of the patient's personality traits, intelligence, and frequency and type of sexual behaviors and has compared these with the same constructs on a normal distribution curve. Ideally, both therapist and patient have reviewed this information and recognized the strengths and weaknesses present. A candid prognosis of the treatment is provided by the therapist and accepted by the patient. They begin and continue the life story treatment with a shared information base about what to expect in terms of challenges and resources.

On the positive side, the identification of a personality trait that is above or below average usually provides a stimulus to explore the etiology and maintenance of the trait. For example, the exhibitionist with a high excitement-seeking trait is invited to see this contribution to his sexual behavior and to see how the excitement-seeking trait will be "honored" when he ceases the sexual exhibitionism. Skydiving anyone? Another example is the patient with very low self-discipline. She poses a risk for both noncompliance with treatment and dropping out of treatment. Both therapist and patient should openly acknowledge this risk and, if possible, have contingencies in place for preventing and responding to relapse using the behavior perspective.

On the negative side, the challenge in integrating the dimension perspective into the life story perspective is the tendency to reify the constructs of *traits* and *intelligence*. Reification is literally "making a thing" out of a construct. Reification tends to concretize the dimensional information, making it seem much more impervious to change than the construct might be. Therapist and patient treat personality traits as unassailable realities that are set in concrete. In fact, if the traits are obtained from self-report inventories, they are part of the life story as it is being worked out by the patient. They are how the person sees himself or herself at the present time. Similarly, it can be helpful to know a valid I.Q. But it is *not* helpful if knowing the I.Q. puts a damper on the development of achievable skills.

One way to prevent reification is to use the results of personality inventories as launching points for the life story therapy rather than as "results" of a "personality test." "You have described yourself as having a high level of interpersonal warmth. How has that shown itself in your life? What has been your response when you have had that need fulfilled? What about when you have been denied it?" Taking such an approach allows patients to remain in control of their story while enriching the vocabulary available to describe it.

CONCLUDING REMARKS

The Perspectives Do Not So Much Answer Questions as Generate Them

It should be clear by this time that the perspectives-informed approach to clinical formulation and treatment of individuals with sexual disorders and dysfunctions is not an answer book or a recipe or a "how to" guide to treating any specific problem. On the contrary, employing a perspectives methodology is likely to generate more questions than the clinician or treatment team would otherwise have considered. Natural, entropic forces tend to work toward an established manner of treating disorders in most clinical settings. A perspectives methodology is counterentropic, challenging clinicians to gather together and explore the one, two, or even three perspectives that may have been collecting dust in their treatment armamentarium.

A perspectives-informed methodology requires clinicians to wrestle with the boundaries of their own ignorance as the "other" perspectives are consulted. This living with unanswered questions is anxiety provoking. It is much easier to have swift, firm, and sure answers or DSM-IV-TR diagnoses for clinical cases — answers usually inadequate to the complexity of the unique patient seeking professional assistance. A perspectives-informed approach to clinical cases is one that can tolerate questions that are not yet answered, because it has a systematic process of attempting to answer those questions. Each perspective guides clinicians to the issues that should be addressed as they formulate the individual case and design the treatment plan.

In many ways, a perspectives-informed methodology is much the same as good research: it knows the limitations of its findings and the tentativeness of its conclusions; it invites further work to answer questions that have arisen in the process. Also like good research, it tends to be fairly simple in design and, when all is said and done, seems to make good common sense.

The Perspectives Require Collegiality

Just as good research usually requires collegiality, so the use of the perspectives in clinical thinking requires clinicians to have and use colleagues. Gone are the days when the mental health practitioner could be an isolated savant. The perspectives methodology requires that the clinician be willing to share expertise with others — especially others who tend to approach cases from one of the other perspectives. The colleagues complement each other with their diverse expertise, just as do the perspectives themselves.

Collegiality comes in many forms. It may be established in a group of peer supervisors, a trusted professional relationship in which each can phone the others for "curbside consultations." It may be set up in the choice of continuing education programs. A perspectives-informed methodology challenges clinicians to choose continuing education programs that address the two or three perspectives in which they most need to expand their knowledge and clinical skills.

Ultimately, of course, clinicians must internalize the collegiality. They must be able to "consult" colleagues without a meeting or phone call. That is, each clinician must be able to review mentally what the colleagues would advise in a particular case. The clinician should conduct an internal dialogue — or conference call, to use a more apt image for the four perspectives — about the particular case. While each perspective will not have the same salience for the formulation of the case, each should be given its collegial respect.

The Perspectives Never Remain Constant

It would be a mistake to think that, once a case is formulated by employing a perspectives methodology, the formulation remains static (e.g., disease primary, life story secondary) until the conclusion of treatment. Every formulation is a hypothesis that is tested in the crucible of therapy and treatment. Often in the course of therapy, new information emerges that calls for a reformulation of the case and the treatment plan. Initially, a major depression may require the disease perspective as the primary treatment perspective. As the depression lifts and psychotherapy gets underway, a traumatic sexual event is reported in therapy. At this point, it is likely that the life story perspective becomes primary while the disease perspective assumes a secondary role. Even at this transition, however, the behavior and dimension perspectives should be reviewed as they may pertain to the patient's life narrative.

The Perspectives Are Conjunctive, Not Disjunctive

One of the limitations of categorical thinking is its disjunctive nature: "either it is an *A* or it is a *B*." But what if "it" has some part *A* and some part *B*? Categorical thinking responds by positing a third category, *C*. The "it" must fit in *A* or *B* or *C*. No other response is possible. This is categorical thinking at its finest. It is not invalid thinking; it merely has the limitation of being disjunctive: there is no blending, no degrees between the categories.

As I hope the preceding chapters have made clear, a perspectives-informed methodology is not disjunctive, with either the disease, dimension, behavior, or life story perspective as the only perspective with which a case can be formulated. The perspectives are conjunctive. They require the clinician to combine elements of various perspectives in the formulation and treatment plan. No clear categorical lines allow for any perspective to be dismissed. To be sure, the perspectives are weighted differently for each case. Each perspective is combined with the others, and in the juxtaposition of the four perspectives the clinician and patient develop an understanding of the problem and a treatment strategy to remedy it.

Finally, the perspectives are conjunctive by inviting into the clinical discussion information and opinions that otherwise might remain isolated. Once these are invited in, clinicians or theorists with such information or opinions are required to give an accounting of themselves. Supporting research and careful elaboration of medical, biographical, and behavioral data will be persuasive; an exclusive certainty of belief will be the death knell of conjunctive conversation. The conjunctive nature of the perspectives methodology means that it is always open ended, looking for new information to test and, if found valid and useful, to add to that which has been integrated thus far.

The Perspectives Entail Completion More than Perfection

Carl Jung wrote of the distinction between psychological completion and psychological perfection.(1) For Jung, *perfection* pertains to the development of the individual: his or her cognitive abilities, psychological life, and personal skills. *Completion,* on the other hand, is the work of relating to others in a manner that provides connectedness and wholeness to the individual. Although both completion and perfection are necessary psychological tasks, there is an inherent tension between the two constructs. In today's culture, that tension is experienced as adults attempt to develop their professional lives and yet maintain and develop relationships with their family members. Perfection wants more career attention; completion speaks for more connectedness with loved ones.

These two constructs offer a final note on the integration of the perspectives. Working with the perspectives methodology is a task clearly in the completion camp. The perspectives challenge us to continue to develop relationships with colleagues who do not share our primary approach to sexual disorders. The perspectives also help us to be more complete in the methodology we use in thinking about sexual disorders and treating them in our patients.

The perspectives' completion bias leaves room, however, for the work of perfection. Perfection as applied here means that individual clinicians must continue to develop their skills in one or two of the perspectives. Psychopharmacologists must endeavor to learn more about the physiological basis of sexual response and the effects of drugs on sexuality. Psychologists who do assessments must continue to develop research and clinical instruments to describe and predict the various trait and cognitive factors involved in sexual behaviors. Cognitive-behaviorists must continue to identify curative factors and strategies in preventing unwanted sexual behaviors or assisting the expression of desired but absent sexual responses. Last, psychotherapists of the various schools — psychoanalytic, object relations, existential — must plumb deeply their heuristic structures and apply them to the sexual problems of today's patients. Each must perfect his or her area of expertise. This is the work of perfection.

Each of these varied professionals, however, must take the results of this perfection work and complete it with dialogue — internal and collegial — with the others. This is the ongoing dialectic. Neither the perfection of specialty skills nor the methodological completion of the perspectives is ever finished. What is required, and what I hope this book has served as an invitation to, is a commitment to take what each of us is perfecting in our specialty and to complete it with the knowledge base and collegial support of the remaining perspectives.

REFERENCES

Chapter 1. Introduction to the Perspectives on Sexual Disorders

1. McHugh PR, Slavney PR. *The Perspectives in Psychiatry,* 2d ed. Baltimore: Johns Hopkins University Press, 1998.

2. Slavney PR. *Perspectives on "Hysteria."* Baltimore: Johns Hopkins University Press, 1990.

3. Neubauer DN. *Understanding Sleeplessness: Perspectives on Insomnia.* Baltimore: Johns Hopkins University Press, 2003.

4. Ghaemi SN. *The Concepts of Psychiatry: Toward Understanding the Mind and Its Pathologies.* Baltimore: Johns Hopkins University Press, 2003.

5. McHugh PR. Managed care and the four perspectives. Paper presented at Academic Behavioral Healthcare Consortium, June 15, 2001.

6. Bancroft J. Sexual science in the 21st century: where are we going? A personal note. *J Sex Res* 1999; 36(3):226–229.

7. Burnett AL, Lowenstein CJ, Bredt DS, Chang TSK, Snyder SH. Nitric oxide: a physiologic mediator of penile erection. *Science* 1992; 257:401–403.

8. Reiss I. Evaluating sexual science. *Annu Rev Sex Res* 1999; 10:236–271.

9. Tiefer L. The medicalization of sexuality: conceptual, normative and professional issues. *Annu Rev Sex Res* 1996; 7:252–282.

10. Adolf Meyer, 1866–1950. In: Winters EE, Bowers AM, editors. *Psychobiology: A Science of Man.* Springfield, Ill.: Charles C Thomas, 1957.

11. Engel GL. The clinical application of the biopsychosocial model. *Am J Psychiatry* 1980; 137:535–544.

12. Engel GL. The need for a new medical model: a challenge for biomedicine. *Science* 1977; 196:129–136.

13. Gatchel RJ. A biopsychosocial overview of pretreatment screening of patients with pain. *Clin J Pain* 2001; 17(3):192–199.

14. Nielson WR, Weir R. Biopsychosocial approaches to the treatment of chronic pain. *Clin J Pain* 2001; 17(4 Suppl):S114–S127.

15. Gabbard GO, Kay J. The fate of integrated treatment: whatever happened to the biopsychosocial psychiatrist? *Am J Psychiatry* 2001; 158:1956–1963.

16. McHugh PR. A structure for psychiatry: how and why to move beyond DSM-IV. *J Nerv Ment Dis* 2003 (in press).

17. Waldstein SR, Neumann SA, Drossman DA, Novack DH. Teaching psychosomatic (biopsychosocial) medicine in United States medical schools: survey findings. *Psychosom Med* 2001; 63(3):335–343.

18. American Psychiatric Association. *Diagnostic and Statistical Manual of Mental Disorders,* 4th ed., text revision ed. Washington, D.C.: American Psychiatric Association, 2000.

19. Hucker SJ. Sexual sadism: psychopathology and theory. In: Laws DR, O'Donohue W, editors. *Sexual Deviance: Theory, Assessment, and Treatment.* New York: Guilford Press, 1997, pp. 194–209.

20. Koss MP, Gidycz CA, Wisniewski N. The scope of rape: incidence and prevalence of sexual aggression and victimization in a national sample of higher education students. *J Consult Clin Psychol* 1987; 55:162–170.

21. Basson R. The female sexual response: a different model. *J Sex Marital Ther* 2000; 26:51–65.

22. Laan E, Everaerd W. Determinants of female sexual arousal: psychological theory and data. *Annu Rev Sex Res* 1995; 6:32–76.

Chapter 2. Sex and the Disease Perspective

1. McHugh PR, Slavney PR. *The Perspectives in Psychiatry,* 2d ed. Baltimore: Johns Hopkins University Press, 1998.

2. Crenshaw TL, Goldberg JP. *Sexual Pharmacology: Drugs That Affect Sexual Function.* New York: W. W. Norton, 1996.

3. Leigh B. The relationship of sex-related alcohol expectancies to alcohol consumption and sexual behavior. *Br J Addict* 1990; 85:919–928.

4. Wilson GT, Lawson DM. Expectancies, alcohol, and sexual arousal in male social drinkers. *J Abnorm Psychol* 1976; 85:587–594.

5. Wilson GT, Lawson DM. The effects of alcohol on sexual arousal in women. *J Abnorm Psychol* 1976; 85:489–497.

6. Moreland RB. Is there a role of hypoxemia in penile fibrosis: a viewpoint presented to the Society for the Study of Impotence. *Int J Impot Res* 1998; 10(2):113–120.

7. Porst H. IC351 (tadalafil, Cialis): update on clinical experience. *Int J Impot Res* 2002; 14(Suppl 1):S57–S64.

8. Schiavi RC, White D, Mandeli J, Levine A. Effects of testosterone administration on sexual behavior and mood in men with erectile dysfunction. *Arch Sex Behav* 1997; 26:231–241.

9. Rowland DL, Greenleaf WJ, Dorfman LJ, Davidson JM. Aging and sexual function in men. *Arch Sex Behav* 1993; 22:545–557.

10. Martin CE. Factors affecting sexual functioning in 60–79-year-old married males. *Arch Sex Behav* 1981; 10:399–420.

11. Schiavi RC. Sexuality and aging in men. *Annu Rev Sex Res* 1990; 1:227–249.

12. Schiavi RC. *Aging and Male Sexuality*. Cambridge: Cambridge University Press, 1999.

13. Laken V, Laken K. *Making Love Again: Hope for Couples Facing Loss of Sexual Intimacy*. Sandwich, Mass.: Ant Hill Press, 2002.

14. Annon J, Robinson CH. The use of vicarious learning in the treatment of sexual concerns. In: LoPiccolo J, LoPiccolo L, editors. *Handbook of Sex Therapy*. New York: Plenum Press, 1978.

15. Shifren JL, Braunstein GD, Simon JA,Simon JA, et al. Transdermal testosterone treatment in women with impaired sexual function after oophorectomy. *N Engl J Med* 2000; 343:682–688.

16. Wincze JP, Carey MP. *Sexual Dysfunction: A Guide for Assessment and Treatment*, 2d ed. New York: Guilford Press, 2001.

17. Maurice WL. *Sexual Medicine in Primary Care*. St. Louis: Mosby, 1999.

18. Fagan PJ, Burnett AL, Rogers L, Schmidt CW. Sexuality and sexual disorders. In: Burton J, Fiebach NH, Kern D, Zieve TP, Ziegelstein R, editors. *Principles of Ambulatory Medicine*. Philadelphia: Lippincott Williams & Wilkins, 2001.

19. Callahan D. *False Hopes: Why America's Quest for Perfect Health Is a Recipe for Failure*. New York: Simon & Schuster, 1998.

Chapter 3. Sex and the Dimension Perspective

1. Kinsey AC, Pomeroy WB, Martin CE. *Sexual Behavior in the Human Male*. Philadelphia: Saunders, 1948.

2. Laumann EO, Gagnon JH, Michael RT, Michaels S. *The Social Organization of Sexuality: Sexual Practices in the United States*. Chicago: University of Chicago Press, 1994.

3. Derogatis LR, Fagan PJ, Strand JG. Sexual disorders measures. In: First MB, editor. *Handbook of Psychiatric Measures*. Washington, D.C.: American Psychiatric Association, 2000, pp. 631–646.

4. Daker-White G. Reliable and valid self-report outcome measures in sexual (dys)function: a systematic review. *Arch Sex Behav* 2002; 31:197–209.

5. Rosen RC, Brown C, Heiman J, et al. The Female Sexual Function Index (FSFI): a multidimensional self-report instrument for the assessment of female sexual function. *J Sex Marital Ther* 2000; 26:191–208.

6. Rosen RC, Riley A, Wagner G, Osterloh IH, Kirkpatrick J, Mishra A. The International Index of Erectile Function (IIEF): a multidimensional scale for assessment of erectile dysfunction. *Urology* 1997; 49:822–830.

7. Rust J, Golombok S. The GRISS: a psychometric instrument for the assessment of sexual dysfunction. *Arch Sex Behav* 1986; 15:153–165.

8. Derogatis LR. The Derogatis Interview for Sexual Functioning. *J Sex Marital Ther* 1997; 23:291–304.

9. Klein F, Sepekoff B, Wolf TJ. Sexual orientation: a multi-variable dynamic process. *J Homosex* 1985; 11(1/2):35–49.

10. Sexual Adjustment Inventory (SAI). Phoenix: Risk and Needs Assessment, 1991.

11. Friedrich WN, Fisher JL, Dittner CA, et al. Child Sexual Behavior Inventory: normative, psychiatric and sexual abuse comparisons. *Child Maltreatment* 2001; 6(1):37–49.

12. Costa PT, McCrae RR. *The NEO-PI-R: Professional Manual*. Odessa, Fla.: Psychological Assessment Resources, 1992.

13. Levin SM, Stava L. Personality characteristics of sex offenders: a review. *Arch Sex Behav* 1987; 16:57–79.

14. Cohen LJ, Gans SW, McGeoch PG, et al. Impulsive personality traits in male pedophiles versus healthy controls: is pedophilia an impulsive-aggressive disorder? *Compr Psychiatry* 2002; 43(2):127–134.

15. Raymond NC, Coleman E, Ohlerking F, Christensen GA, Miner M. Psychiatric comorbidity in pedophilic sex offenders. *Am J Psychiatry* 1999; 156:786–788.

16. Costa PT, Fagan PJ, Piedmont RL, Ponticas Y, Wise TN. The Five-Factor Model of personality and sexual functioning in outpatient men and women. *Psychiatr Med* 1992; 10:199–215.

17. Fagan PJ, Wise TN, Schmidt CW, Ponticas Y, Marshall RD, Costa PT. A comparison of five-factor personality dimensions in males with sexual dysfunction and males with paraphilia. *J Pers Assess* 1991; 57(3):434–448.

18. Conte JR, Wolf S, Smith T. What sexual offenders tell us about prevention strategies. *Child Abuse Negl* 1989; 13:293–301.

19. Quinsey VL, Harris GT, Rice ME, Cormier, CA. Sex offenders. In *Violent Offenders: Appraising and Managing Risk*. Washington, D.C.: American Psychological Association, 1998, pp. 119–137.

20. Halpern CT, Joyner K, Udry JR, Suchindran C. Smart teens don't have sex (or kiss much either). *J Adolesc Health* 2000; 26(3):213–225.

21. Sandler AD, Watson TE, Levine MD. A study of the cognitive aspects of sexual decision making in adolescent females. *J Dev Behav Pediatr* 1992; 13(2):202–207.

22. Weiss P. [Psychological predictors of recidivism in sex offenders] (in Czech). *Cesk Psychiatr* 1989; 85(4):250–255.

23. Van Bourgodien ME, Reichle NC, Palmer A. Sexual behavior in adults with autism. *J Autism Dev Disord* 1997; 27(2):113–125.

24. Kohn Y, Fahum T, Ratzoni G, Apter A. Aggression and sexual offense in Asperger's syndrome. *Isr J Psychiatry Relat Sci* 1998; 35(4):293–299.

25. Realmuto GM, Ruble LA. Sexual behaviors in autism: problems of definition and management. *J Autism Dev Disord* 1999; 29(2):121–127.

26. Fagan PJ, Strand JG. A call for non-proprietary peer-reviewed research. *J Sex Marital Ther* 2001; 27:141–143.

27. McConaghy N. *Sexual Behavior: Problems and Management*. New York: Plenum Press, 1993.

28. Weinrich JD, Snyder PJ, Pillard RC, et al. A factor analysis of the Klein Sexual Orientation Grid in two disparate samples. *Arch Sex Behav* 1993; 22:157–168.

Chapter 4. Sex and the Behavior Perspective

1. Goodman A. Sexual addiction: designation and treatment. *J Sex Marital Ther* 1992; 18:303–314.

2. Halpern CT, Udry JR, Suchindran C. Testosterone predicts initiation of coitus in adolescent females. *Psychosom Med* 1997; 59(2):161–171.

3. Halpern CT, Udry JR, Suchindran C. Monthly measures of salivary testosterone predict sexual activity in adolescent males. *Arch Sex Behav* 1998; 27:445–465.

4. Shifren JL, Braunstein GD, Simon JA, et al. Transdermal testosterone treatment in women with impaired sexual function after oophorectomy. *N Engl J Med* 2000; 343:682–688.

5. Schiavi RC. *Aging and Male Sexuality.* Cambridge: Cambridge University Press, 1999.

6. Campbell BC, Udry JR. Implications of hormonal influences on sexual behavior for demographic models of reproduction. *Ann N Y Acad Sci* 2002; 18(709):117–127.

7. Bradford JM, McLean D. Sexual offenders, violence and testosterone: a clinical study. *Can J Psychiatry* 1984; 29(4):335–343.

8. Seim HC, Dwyer M. Evaluation of serum testosterone and luteinizing hormone levels in sex offenders. *Fam Pract Res J* 1988; 7(3):175–180.

9. Stein DJ, Black DW, Shapira NA, Spitzer RL. Hypersexual disorder and preoccupation with internet pornography. *Am J Psychiatry* 2001; 158:1590–1594.

10. Laumann EO, Gagnon JH, Michael RT, Michaels S. *The Social Organization of Sexuality: Sexual Practices in the United States.* Chicago: University of Chicago Press, 1994.

11. Jaspers K. *General Psychopathology.* Baltimore: Johns Hopkins University Press, 1997.

12. Slavney PR. *Perspectives on "Hysteria."* Baltimore: Johns Hopkins University Press, 1990.

13. Cox BJ, Borger SC, Asmundson GJ, Taylor S. Dimensions of hypochondriasis and the five-factor model of personality. *Pers Individual Differences* 2000; 29:99–108.

14. Friederich EG. Therapeutic studies on vulvar vestibulitis. *J Reprod Med* 1988; 33(6):514–518.

15. Meana M, Binik YM, Khalife S, Cohen DR. Biopsychosocial profile of women with dyspareunia. *Obstet Gynecol* 1997; 90:583–589.

16. Van Lankveld JJ, Weijenborg PT, Ter Kuile MM. Psychological profiles of and sexual function in women with vulvar vestibulitis and their partners. *Obstet Gynecol* 2001; 88:65–70.

Chapter 5. Treatment of Sexual Disorders in the Behavior Perspective

1. Masters WH, Johnson VE. *Human Sexual Inadequacy.* New York: Little, Brown, 1970.

2. Wincze JP, Carey MP. *Sexual Dysfunction: A Guide for Assessment and Treatment,* 2d ed. New York: Guilford Press, 2001.

3. Leiblum SR, Rosen RC. *Principles and Practice of Sex Therapy,* 3d ed. New York: Guilford Press, 2000.

4. Kaplan HS. *The New Sex Therapy.* New York: Brunner/Mazel, 1974.

5. Hawton K. *Sex Therapy: A Practical Guide.* Northvale, N.J.: Aronson, 1985.

6. Heiman JR, Meston C. Empirically validated treatment for sexual dysfunction. *Annu Rev Sex Res* 1997; 8:148–194.

7. Moeller FG, Barratt ES, Dougherty DM, Schmitz JM, Swann AC. Psychiatric aspects of impulsivity. *Am J Psychiatry* 2001; 158:1783–1793.

8. Laumann EO, Gagnon JH, Michael RT, Michaels S. *The Social Organization of Sexuality: Sexual Practices in the United States.* Chicago: University of Chicago Press, 1994.

9. Prochaska JD, Norcross JC, DiClemente CG. *Changing for Good.* New York: HarperCollins, 1994.

10. Bradford JM. The treatment of sexual deviation using a pharmacological approach. *J Sex Res* 2000; 37(3):248–257.

11. Kafka MP, Prentky R. Fluoxetine treatment of nonparaphilic sexual addictions and paraphilias in men. *J Clin Psychiatry* 1992; 53:351–358.

12. Gottesman HG, Shubert DS. Low-dose oral medroxyprogesterone acetate in the management of the paraphilias. *J Clin Psychiatry* 1993; 54:182–188.

13. Bradford JM, Pawlak A. Effects of cyproterone acetate on sexual arousal patterns of pedophiles. *Arch Sex Behav* 1993; 22:629–641.

14. Krueger RB, Kaplan MS. Depot-leuprolide acetate for treatment of paraphilias: a report of twelve cases. *Arch Sex Behav* 2001; 30:409–422.

15. Federoff JP. Buspirone in the treatment of transvestitic fetishism. *J Clin Psychiatry* 1988; 48:408–409.

16. Grant JE, Kim SW. A case of kleptomania and compulsive sexual behavior treated with naltrexone. *Ann Clin Psychiatry* 2002; 13(4):229–231.

17. Kamel HK. Sexuality in aging: focus on institutionalized elderly. *Ann Long Term Care* 2001; 9(5):64–72.

18. DeLamater JD, Hyde JS. Essentialism versus social constructionism in the study of human sexuality. *J Sex Res* 1998; 35(1):10–18.

Chapter 6. Sex and the Life Story Perspective

1. Jaspers K. *General Psychopathology,* vol. 1. Baltimore: Johns Hopkins University Press, 1997.

2. Scharff DE. *The Sexual Relationship: An Object Relations View of Sex and the Family.* New York: Routledge, 1982.

3. Stoller RJ. *Presentations of Gender.* New Haven: Yale University Press, 1985.

4. Freund K. A conceptual framework for the study of anomalous erotic preferences. *J Sex Marital Ther* 1978; 4:3–10.

5. Freund K, Scher H, Hucker S. The courtship disorders. *Arch Sex Behav* 1983; 12:369–379.

6. Freund K, Scher H, Hucker S. The courtship disorders: a further investigation. *Arch Sex Behav* 1984; 13:133–140.

7. Berger P, Luckman T. *The Social Construction of Reality: A Treatise in the Sociology of Knowledge.* Garden City, N.Y.: Doubleday, 1966.

8. DeLamater JD, Hyde JS. Essentialism versus social constructionism in the study of human sexuality. *J Sex Res* 1998; 35(1):10–18.

9. Colapinto J. *As Nature Made Him.* New York: HarperCollins, 1999.

10. Zucker KJ. Biological influences on psychosocial differentiation. In: Unger RK, editor. *Handbook of the Psychology of Women and Gender.* New York: Wiley, 2001, pp. 101–115.

11. Gagnon JH. The explicit and implicit use of the scripting perspective in sex research. *Annu Rev Sex Res* 1990; 1:1–43.

12. Laquer T. *Making Sex: Body and Gender from the Greeks to Freud.* Cambridge: Harvard University Press, 1990.

13. Frankl V. *Man's Search for Meaning,* 2d ed. New York: Washington Square Press, 1984.

Chapter 7. Integrating the Perspectives

1. Jung CG. Answer to Job. In: Read H, Fordham M, Adler G, McGuire W, editors. *Psychology and Religion: West and East.* Princeton: Princeton University Press, 1969, pp. 365–470.

INDEX

About the Author

Peter J. Fagan is an associate professor of medical psychology in the Department of Psychiatry and Behavioral Sciences at the Johns Hopkins University School of Medicine. A clinical psychologist, Dr. Fagan has been director of the Sexual Behaviors Consultation Unit and the Center for Sexual and Marital Health at Hopkins since 1987. This unit received the Award for Creativity in Psychiatric Education (Honorable Mention) from the American College of Psychiatrists in February 2000.

Dr. Fagan has served as president of the Society for Sexual Therapy and Research and is a member of the International Academy of Sex Research. He is the author of several chapters on sexuality in medical textbooks and of research articles on the clinical characteristics of persons with sexual disorders.